# Hepatitis

# Hepatitis

## Melissa Abramovitz

**LUCENT BOOKS**

*A part of Gale, Cengage Learning*

GALE
CENGAGE Learning

Detroit • New York • San Francisco • New Haven, Conn • Waterville, Maine • London

LIBRARY OF CONGRESS CATALOGING-IN-PUBLICATION DATA

Abramovitz, Melissa, 1954-
 Hepatitis / by Melissa Abramovitz.
    p. cm. -- (Diseases & disorders)
 Includes bibliographical references and index.
 ISBN 978-1-4205-0595-5 (hardcover)
 1. Hepatitis--Juvenile literature. I. Title.
 RC848.H42A24 2011
 616.3'623--dc22

                                                          2010050807

Lucent Books
27500 Drake Rd
Farmington Hills MI 48331

ISBN-13: 978-1-4205-0595-5
ISBN-10: 1-4205-0595-5

Printed in the United States of America
1 2 3 4 5 6 7 15 14 13 12 11

Printed by Bang Printing, Brainerd, MN, 1st Ptg., 06/2011

# Table of Contents

# "The Most Difficult Puzzles Ever Devised"

**C**harles Best, one of the pioneers in the search of a cure for diabetes, once explained what it is about medical research that intrigued him so. "It's not just the gratification of knowing one is helping people," he confided, "although that probably is a more heroic and selfless motivation. Those feelings may enter in, but truly, what I find best is the feeling of going toe to toe with nature, of trying to solve the most difficult puzzles ever devised. The answers are there somewhere, those keys that will solve the puzzle and make the patient well. But how will those keys be found?"

Since the dawn of civilization, nothing has so puzzled people—and often frightened them, as well—as the onset of illness in a body or mind that had seemed healthy before. A seizure, the inability of a heart to pump, the sudden deterioration of muscle tone in a small child – being unable to reverse such conditions or even to understand why they occur was unspeakably frustrating to healers. Even before there were names for such conditions, even before they were understood at all, each was a reminder of how complex the human body was, and how vulnerable.

While our grappling with understanding diseases has been frustrating at times, it has also provided some of humankind's most heroic accomplishments. Alexander Fleming's accidental discovery in 1928 of a mold that could be turned into penicillin has resulted in the saving of untold millions of lives. The isolation of the enzyme insulin has reversed what was once a death sentence for anyone with diabetes. There have been great strides in combating conditions for which there is not yet a cure, too. Medicines can help AIDS patients live longer, diagnostic tools such as mammography and ultrasounds can help doctors find tumors while they are treatable, and laser surgery techniques have made the most intricate, minute operations routine.

This "toe-to-toe" competition with diseases and disorders is even more remarkable when seen in a historical continuum. An astonishing amount of progress has been made in a very short time. Just two hundred years ago, the existence of germs as a cause of some diseases was unknown. In fact, it was less than 150 years ago that a British surgeon named Joseph Lister had difficulty persuading his fellow doctors that washing their hands before delivering a baby might increase the chances of a healthy delivery (especially if they had just attended to a diseased patient)!

Each book in Lucent's Diseases and Disorders series explores a disease or disorder and the knowledge that has been accumulated (or discarded) by doctors through the years. Each book also examines the tools used for pinpointing a diagnosis, as well as the various means that are used to treat or cure a disease. Finally, new ideas are presented – techniques or medicines that may be on the horizon.

Frustration and disappointment are still part of medicine, for not every disease or condition can be cured or prevented. But the limitations of knowledge are being pushed outward constantly; the "most difficult puzzles ever devised" are finding challengers every day.

# Hepatitis: A Frightening Disease

**H**epatitis, or inflammation of the liver, is a frightening disease for many reasons. For one thing, anyone of any age can get hepatitis, and its severity and outcome vary widely among individuals. No one with hepatitis knows whether he or she will become seriously ill or whether they will recover or die from the illness. Singer Steven Tyler of the rock band Aerosmith, for example, was cured of the form of the disease called hepatitis C after undergoing a year of grueling treatment. Baseball superstar Mickey Mantle, on the other hand, died of the liver cancer that can result from chronic, or long-term hepatitis. Chronic hepatitis is, in fact, the leading cause of liver cancer and liver transplantation in the United States.

Another frightening aspect of hepatitis is the fact that several of its nine types are highly contagious. The virus that causes hepatitis B, for instance, is one hundred times more contagious than the AIDS (Acquired Immune Deficiency Syndrome) virus. Hepatitis B virus can also live for more than a week outside the body and can infect people who come in contact with it.

The reality that more than a billion people throughout the world have hepatitis, and that millions die each year as a result, is also frightening. Some areas of the world are affected more than others, but hepatitis exists everywhere. For example, more than 10 percent of the population in the countries of Bolivia, Burundi, Cameroon, Guinea, Mongolia, Rwanda, and Tanzania,

Several hundred victims and health advocates march and rally to raise awareness of hepatitis C.

and 25 percent of the population in Egypt and the former Soviet Union are infected with hepatitis C alone. In the United States, about 3.2 million people have hepatitis C, and health officials expect the death rate from the disease to quadruple in the next ten years.

## A Silent Killer

One of the scariest things about hepatitis is that people with the disease often show no symptoms and do not know they are infected. For instance, 50–70 percent of adults and children over age five with early-stage hepatitis B and 70 percent of children under age six with hepatitis A have no symptoms. People with contagious forms of hepatitis can spread the disease to others whether or not they have symptoms, and each year millions are infected by disease carriers who are unaware that they are sick. In addition, some types of hepatitis can hide in the liver for twenty or thirty years and cause serious damage, while the affected individual remains unaware of the problem. By the time symptoms become apparent and a doctor diagnoses the illness, the damage may be irreversible and even deadly.

The devastating consequences of not being aware of a hepatitis infection have led public health agencies such as the Institute of Medicine to warn the public that "Chronic viral hepatitis is a silent killer."[1] Other forms of hepatitis, such as alcoholic and toxic hepatitis, can be silent killers as well.

## Widespread Ignorance

Besides widespread unawareness of infection, many people are ignorant about the risks of getting hepatitis and of how to prevent it. Although anyone can contract hepatitis, certain people are at higher risk for certain forms. People who live in or travel to areas with poor sanitation, for example, are at greatest risk for hepatitis A and E, but many do not take precautions like getting vaccinated against hepatitis A or avoiding raw foods in these areas. Illegal drug users, health care workers, and people who engage in promiscuous sex are at high risk for hepatitis B, but, again, many do not take precautions to prevent contracting or spreading the disease because they do not know about the risks.

A 2010 report on viral hepatitis by the Institute of Medicine concluded that "There is a lack of knowledge and awareness about chronic viral hepatitis on the part of the health-care and social-service providers, among at-risk populations, members of the public and policy makers."[2] Because of the need to educate everyone, including health care professionals, about hepatitis, public health agencies and nonprofit foundations throughout the world have made allocating funding for education a priority. In addition, these agencies are conducting extensive research to better understand, prevent, and treat hepatitis.

Legislators and public health agencies in the United States have responded to these needs by launching outreach and research programs they believe can lessen the burden of this frightening disease in the future. In 2001 the Centers for Disease Control (CDC) developed a National Hepatitis B and C Prevention Strategy that emphasizes education and improved

Senator John Kerry (D-Mass.) introduced the Viral Hepatitis and Liver Cancer Control and Prevention Act of 2010, which calls for a national strategy to prevent and control hepatitis B and C.

tracking, or surveillance. This program has been moderately successful in increasing awareness, but experts say more needs to be done. Thus, in August of 2010, Senator John Kerry introduced legislation called the Viral Hepatitis and Liver Cancer Control and Prevention Act of 2010 to augment existing efforts. This would provide nearly $600 million to fund a national plan for prevention, control, and treatment. In a speech about the trauma and dangers of hepatitis, Kerry said, "We can easily avoid these needless tragedies with prevention, surveillance programs, and by educating Americans about this deadly disease. The bill I'm introducing today will help create a national strategy to combat and prevent hepatitis, hopefully ending this silent affliction's often deadly consequences."[3]

# CHAPTER ONE

# What Is Hepatitis?

**H**epatitis is inflammation, or swelling, of the liver. The term *hepatitis* comes from the Latin words *hep*, meaning liver, and *titus*, meaning inflammation. There are several types of hepatitis that vary in duration, severity, and other characteristics, but all share the basic quality of liver inflammation.

Scientists believe that all types of hepatitis have existed in humans for thousands of years, but doctors did not identify the various types until they possessed the technology for viewing and analyzing microscopic cells and submicroscopic viruses. The types of hepatitis include five kinds of viral hepatitis (A, B, C, D, and E), autoimmune hepatitis, alcoholic hepatitis, nonalcoholic fatty liver–induced hepatitis (also called nonalcoholic steatohepatitis), and toxic hepatitis. Viral hepatitis is the most common form of the disease.

In addition to categorizing hepatitis by type, doctors also refer to the length of time a person has had the disease. Acute, or short-term, hepatitis lasts six months or less, while the chronic, or long-term, form lasts longer than six months. All types of hepatitis can be acute, but only B, C, D, autoimmune, alcoholic, nonalcoholic steatohepatitis, and toxic hepatitis can be chronic.

All types of hepatitis can also be fulminant. This refers to a very severe, life-threatening form of acute hepatitis that often results in liver failure and death.

| 9 Types of Hepatitis | | |
|---|---|---|
| **Type – Viral** | **Acute** | **Chronic** |
| 1. **Hepatitis A (HAV)** Formerly known as infectious hepatitis, HAV is a normally minor form of hepatitis caused by an RNA virus that does not persist in the blood. It is usually transmitted by ingestion of contaminated food or water. | ● | |
| 2. **Hepatitis B (HBV)** HBV is a form of hepatitis caused by a DNA virus that persists in the blood, characterized by a long incubation period. It is usually transmitted by sexual contact or by injection or ingestion of infected blood or other bodily fluids. | ● | ● |
| 3. **Hepatitis C (HCV)** HCV is a form of hepatitis with clinical effects similar to those of hepatitis B, caused by a blood-borne retrovirus (hepatitis C virus) that may be of the hepatitis non-A, non-B type. | ● | ● |
| 4. **Hepatitis D (HDV)** Also called delta hepatitis, HDV is a form of hepatitis that is similar to hepatitis B and is caused by coinfection with the hepatitis B virus and hepatitis D virus. | ● | ● |
| 5. **Hepatitis E (HEV)** HEV is a hepatitis that is rare in the United States but is common in some third-world countries, is usually contracted from sewage-contaminated water, and is caused by a highly variable single-stranded RNA virus. | ● | |
| **Type – Nonviral** | **Acute** | **Chronic** |
| 6. **Autoimmune Hepatitis (AIH)** Also called lupoid hepatitis, AIH is a form of hepatitis caused by the body's immune system attacking the liver. | ● | ● |
| 7. **Toxic Hepatitis** Also called drug hepatitis, toxic hepatitis results from ingestion or exposure to certain drugs or poisons. | ● | ● |
| 8. **Alcoholic Hepatitis** An inflammation of the liver due to excessive intake of alcohol. | ● | ● |
| 9. **Nonalcoholic Steatohepatitis** A liver that contains fatty deposits and shows evidence of inflammation but has not been damaged by alcohol. | ● | ● |

Source: www.cdc.gov/hepatitis/

# Hepatitis A

Hepatitis A, or HAV, used to be known as infectious hepatitis. It can last for several weeks to several months and can be mild or severe, but most people recover fully from it. Only one-half of 1 percent of infected people die from liver failure brought on by HAV. Most of those who die are over age fifty. Those who recover cannot become reinfected later on because their immune systems make antibodies against the virus. Antibodies are chemicals produced by the immune system to fight specific antigens, or foreign substances. These antibodies remain in the body indefinitely.

Although most people recover from HAV, health experts still consider it to be a serious illness that brings much suffering and hardship. According to the World Health Organization (WHO), "The disease can wreak significant economic and social consequences in communities. It can take weeks or months for people recovering from the illness to return to work, school, or daily life."[4]

WHO estimates that there are about 1.4 million new cases of HAV diagnosed each year throughout the world. About 25,000 new infections occur each year in the United States.

Epidemics of HAV occur sporadically around the world and can affect hundreds of thousands of people at a time. For example, a 1988 epidemic in China sickened more than 300,000 people.

## Hepatitis B

Hepatitis B, or HBV, can be acute or chronic. As the authors of *The Cleveland Clinic Guide to Liver Disorders* explain, "Researchers aren't sure why some acute HBV patients are able to expel the virus from their bodies, while others are not, but it appears that the immune system is better at eliminating HBV in adults than in children."[5] Indeed, 90–95 percent of infants with HBV go on to develop the chronic form, compared to 65–75 percent of children and 5 percent of adults. Studies have shown that people who drink alcohol or smoke cigarettes are also more likely to develop chronic HBV.

Chronic HBV is much more likely than acute HBV to lead to complications like liver scarring (fibrosis), severe scarring called cirrhosis, liver cancer, and liver failure. Of people with chronic HBV, 15–25 percent die from liver failure, while about 1 percent of those with acute HBV succumb to complications.

About 1.2 million people in the United States and more than 350 million worldwide currently have chronic HBV, and more than one million die each year from the disease. The Centers for Disease Control (CDC) estimates that each year an additional 43,000 people in the United States become infected.

## Hepatitis C

Hepatitis C, or HCV, used to be called non-A, non-B hepatitis. About 170 million people worldwide and 3.2 million in the United States had chronic HCV as of 2010. Of people infected with acute HCV, 70–80 percent go on to develop the chronic form, and 60–70 percent with chronic HCV develop severe complications over ten to thirty or more years. Those who drink alcohol, smoke, are obese, or contract the disease before age forty are most likely to develop these complications. Having chronic HCV is the leading reason for people needing liver

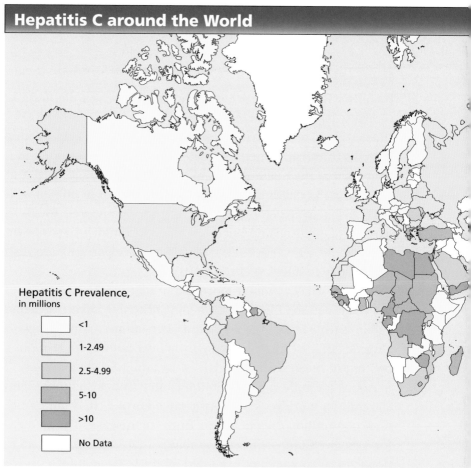

### Hepatitis C around the World

Hepatitis C Prevalence, in millions

- <1
- 1-2.49
- 2.5-4.99
- 5-10
- >10
- No Data

Source: Adapted from www.hepatitis.org/hepcslides/POWERPOI.PPT/01PVANDA/sld005.h

transplants in the United States, and about 15,000 Americans die from HCV each year.

## Hepatitis D and E

Hepatitis D, or HDV or delta hepatitis, is uncommon in the United States, but it affects about 15 million people worldwide. Areas with the highest incidence include southern Italy, north Africa, the Middle East, South America, and certain South Pacific islands.

Only people infected with HBV can get hepatitis D. Acute and chronic cases range from mild to severe, and doctors do not know how many infections result in liver failure and death, since it would be difficult to determine whether a death resulted from HBV or HDV.

Hepatitis E (HEV) can only be acute. Either the infected person fights off the virus and recovers, or the virus kills him or her within six months. HEV, like HAV, does not take up long-term residence in the liver.

Like hepatitis D, HEV is rarely seen in the United States but is common elsewhere. WHO estimates that one-third of the world's population has been infected with HEV. Epidemics have occurred in Asia, the Middle East, Africa, and Central America. Most infected Americans contract the disease during travel to these areas.

One-half to 4 percent of people infected with hepatitis E die from it. However, this percentage rises dramatically for pregnant women; for 20–45 percent of infected pregnant women the disease is fatal.

# Hepatitis Serology Tests to Diagnose Types of Viral Hepatitis

Doctors diagnose hepatitis A with a blood test that measures IgM (immunoglobulin M) antibodies against HAV. IgM antibodies are the first type of antibody the body makes in response to an infection.

Hepatitis B is diagnosed with one or all of several standard tests that measure either antigens (proteins in the virus) or antibodies the patient makes to these antigens. Tests include: IgM or IgG anti-HBc (antibodies to hepatitis B core antigen), HBsAG (hepatitis B virus surface antigen), anti-HBs (antibody to hepatitis B surface antigen), and HBeAG (a form of hepatitis B virus core antigen that appears in blood only when the virus is actively replicating). These tests can reveal whether an HBV infection is acute or chronic, since different antigens and antibodies appear in the blood at different stages of the disease.

Tests for Hepatitis C include anti-HCV (measures antibodies to HCV) and HCV RNA polymerase chain reaction (detects RNA found in the HCV virus). HCV RNA can be detected with techniques known as enzyme-linked immunosorbent assay (ELISA) or recombinant immunoblot assay (RIBA). These techniques can tell doctors which of several subtypes of the hepatitis C virus a person has.

Hepatitis D and E can be diagnosed with tests that measure IgM antibodies to the viruses or by tests that detect the viruses. However, the viral detection tests are only available at a limited number of research laboratories.

## Coinfection

People can be infected with more than one hepatitis virus. Doctors refer to these individuals as coinfected. Everyone with hepatitis D is co-infected with HBV. Anywhere from 9–30 percent of people with all types of hepatitis are coinfected with HBV and HCV. People can also be coinfected with viral and nonviral hepatitis. Any sort of coinfection increases the chances of severe disease and unfavorable outcomes.

## Nonviral Forms of Hepatitis

Autoimmune hepatitis (AIH) is one type of nonviral hepatitis. The Swedish doctor Jan Waldenstrom first described AIH in 1950. Doctors at first thought AIH was a form of the autoimmune disease lupus and initially called it lupoid hepatitis, but they later realized it was an entirely different disease. Autoimmune diseases occur when the body's immune system attacks its own tissues. In AIH, it is the liver cells.

Experts believe AIH affects one in 100,000 people worldwide. Of this number, 70 percent are females between the ages of fifteen and forty. There are three subtypes of AIH. Type 1 usually affects women who have another autoimmune disease such as type 1 diabetes or Crohn's disease. Type 2 is less common and usually strikes girls ages two to fourteen. Type 3 is similar to type 1 AIH, but affected people lack the auto (self) antibodies found in the blood of those with types 1 and 2. Most cases of all three types are chronic and can result in serious liver damage.

Toxic or drug-induced hepatitis results from ingestion or exposure to certain drugs or poisons. It can be acute or chronic. Public health agencies do not keep statistics on the prevalence and death rate of the acute and chronic forms, but experts believe that thousands of people are affected by toxic hepatitis each year.

Alcoholic hepatitis is similar to toxic hepatitis in that it results from the toxic effects of a substance (in this case alcohol), but doctors classify it as a separate type of hepatitis. Experts estimate that more than two million people in the United States suffer from acute or chronic alcoholic hepatitis, but the true number is likely to be much higher since many remain undiagnosed. The term *alcoholic hepatitis* can also be misleading because not everyone who gets the disease is an alcoholic (someone who abuses and is dependent on alcohol).

Of the estimated 100,000 people affected by autoimmune hepatitis worldwide, 70 percent are females between the ages of 15 and 40.

Social drinkers and binge drinkers who may not be considered to be alcoholics can also develop alcoholic hepatitis. The disease usually develops after alcohol induces a condition of excess fat buildup in the liver (called fatty liver), and the liver becomes inflamed. Both the acute and chronic forms can lead to liver failure.

Nonalcoholic fatty liver disease (NAFLD) is a fatty liver in people who do not drink much alcohol. The National Institute of Diabetes and Digestive and Kidney Diseases (NIDDK) estimates that 10–20 percent of Americans have NAFLD. Many, but not all, are obese or have diabetes. Doctors say NAFLD itself is not harmful to the liver, but when it progresses to nonalcoholic steatohepatitis (NASH) and the liver becomes inflamed, this can result in scarring, liver cancer, or liver failure. One in four people with NAFLD develops NASH, and about nine million Americans have this form of hepatitis.

## What Does the Liver Do?

All types of hepatitis can affect overall health and even survival because the liver is one of the most important organs in
the body. It is about the size of a football, making it the largest
internal organ, and sits in the upper right quadrant of the abdomen under the ribcage. According to the authors of *The Cleveland Clinic Guide to Liver Disorders,*

> The liver performs more than 500 functions that keep
> the human body working efficiently. Without a liver, our
> blood would be clogged with fats, glucosesugar, and
> amino acidsproteins. Our bodies would have no defense
> against infections, no way to eliminate the drugs and
> toxins we consume, and no mechanism for processing
> digested food from the intestine.[6]

The liver also manufactures blood clotting factors, hor-
mones, immune system chemicals, bile (a chemical compound
that digests fats), and albumin (a protein needed for proper
fluid balance).

The liver performs its functions through the veins and arter-
ies that transport blood to it and by means of specialized cells
called hepatocytes that make up its structure. About 25 percent
of the blood in the body passes through the liver every minute.
The blood reaches the liver through the portal vein and the
hepatic artery. The portal vein runs from the intestines to the
liver. Blood that enters the liver through this vein has already
absorbed nutrients, toxins, drugs, and other substances from
the intestines. Thus, the liver is the first organ to receive these
substances after the intestines absorb them, and it plays a big
role in processing them before they reach other organs.

The hepatic artery goes directly from the lungs and heart to
the liver. Blood in the hepatic artery is filled with the oxygen
needed by all cells in the body to stay alive. The blood from the
portal vein and the hepatic artery mix once inside the liver, and
this mixed blood flows through small blood vessels called sinu-
soids. Nutrients, drugs, and toxins pass through the sinusoid

# Liver Biopsies

Doctors can perform three types of liver biopsies. Each is done while the patient is sedated to minimize pain. In a percutaneous biopsy, the physician makes a small incision and inserts a hollow needle through the abdomen into the liver after determining the correct location using ultrasound imaging. Ultrasound uses sound waves to create video screen images of internal organs. After withdrawing the needle with a liver sample, the doctor sews up the incision and the patient must remain on his or her right side for about two hours to reduce bleeding.

A doctor will perform a transvenous biopsy when the patient has excess fluid in the abdomen or if his or her blood clots slowly. The physician makes a small incision in the side of the neck and inserts a hollow tube called a sheath into the jugular vein. After injecting a dye that lights up on an X-ray machine, the doctor guides the sheath down the jugular vein into one of the liver veins and passes a biopsy needle through the sheath into the liver to withdraw a tissue sample. After the incision is closed, the patient is monitored for four to six hours.

When a doctor wishes to obtain one or more samples from specific areas of the liver, a laparoscopic biopsy is performed. Here, plastic tube-like instruments called cannulas and tiny lighted video cameras are passed through one or more tiny incisions in the abdomen. The doctor infuses a special gas through the cannula to inflate the abdomen so there is room to work, then inserts a biopsy needle to remove liver samples. The patient must rest for a few hours afterward.

walls and enter the hepatocytes, which metabolize and detoxify these substances and also manufacture important chemicals. The hepatocytes then return the blood to the hepatic artery, which takes the blood to the vena cava, one of two large veins that lead to the heart. Waste products from the liver go to the kidneys to be excreted in the urine or through the bile ducts that take bile to the intestines.

## The Importance of the Liver

People cannot live without a functioning liver, and when inflammation from hepatitis leads to a large number of hepatocytes that cannot work properly or that die, liver failure and death result. The inflammation can also provoke the abnormal cell growth that characterizes liver cancer and can cause scarring or cirrhosis, which further impact the ability of the liver to function. Although a healthy liver can regenerate if part of it is removed or damaged, a cirrhotic liver generally cannot heal, regenerate, or perform its duties.

A poorly functioning liver may not produce any symptoms until it is close to failing, as explained by Hepatitis Foundation International, "The trouble is, your liver is a silent partner; when something's wrong it does not complain until the damage

The liver is a vital organ that has a wide range of functions, including detoxification, protein synthesis, and production of biochemicals necessary for digestion.

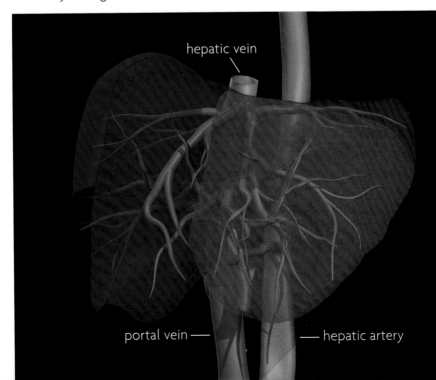

hepatic vein

portal vein —            — hepatic artery

is far advanced."[7] This is not always true, though; sometimes symptoms appear before irreversible damage occurs.

## Typical Symptoms

In types of hepatitis that are strictly acute, the likelihood of any symptoms at all seems to be related to the age of the infected person. For example, 70 percent of children under age six with hepatitis A show no symptoms, while 80 percent of older children and adults do have symptoms. With chronic forms of the disease, the longer the individual has hepatitis, the more likely they are to show symptoms.

Symptoms, when they do occur, appear anywhere from a week to months or years after exposure to the virus in cases of viral hepatitis, depending on the incubation period of the particular virus. An incubation period is the time between when infection occurs and symptoms appear. The incubation period for HAV, for example, is ten to fifty days, while that for HCV is four to twelve weeks. With nonviral hepatitis, symptoms sometimes show up immediately after onset of the disease and other times not for many years.

The symptoms for all types of hepatitis are very similar and may include fever, fatigue, loss of appetite, nausea, vomiting, abdominal pain, abdominal swelling, muscle wasting, an odd taste in the mouth, dark-colored urine, clay-colored bowel movements, mental confusion, joint pain, jaundice (yellowish tinge in the skin and whites of the eyes), and sometimes red palms or spider veins on the skin from internal bleeding. In addition, people with alcoholic or toxic hepatitis may show sweating, convulsions, or coma from a drug overdose.

The number and severity of symptoms varies widely among individuals. David, who had HBV, for instance, experienced extreme fatigue and dizziness and found himself getting lost when going to familiar places. Joanna, who also had HBV, noticed that food did not taste good and lost her appetite. One woman with autoimmune hepatitis described her symptoms as: "Always feeling fatigued, lots of upper right quadrant pain

The yellowing symptoms of jaundice are caused by an excess of bilirubin, a bile pigment, in the blood.

and nausea. It feels like someone is stabbing your liver all day long."[8]

As liver expert Melissa Palmer explains in *Dr. Melissa Palmer's Guide to Hepatitis & Liver Disease,*

> Fatigue is probably the most common and debilitating symptom of liver disease... The liver's job is to keep the right amount of glucose in the blood and to keep it flowing to the organs that need it at all times. If your liver is inflamed or damaged, your body will have trouble regulating the glucose levels in your blood. This is one of the reasons that so many people with liver disease tire so easily.[9]

Fatigue can also result from the buildup of toxins when a diseased liver cannot process them.

Toxin buildup can also lead to mental confusion or even coma, especially when the poison that accumulates is ammonia, which is highly toxic to the brain. When this happens, doctors refer to it as hepatic encephalopathy (liver-induced brain inflammation). In addition, toxins can result in symptoms such as nausea and lack of appetite, or these symptoms may be due to an inflamed liver pressing against the stomach.

Jaundice results from a diseased liver's inability to remove a chemical called bilirubin from the blood. Bilirubin comes from by-products of dead red blood cells. It is normally excreted in the yellowish-green bile, but when the liver cannot produce enough bile or its flow is interrupted, bilirubin may appear in the skin and eyes, making them appear yellow. Without adequate bile, the body also cannot digest the fats it needs to absorb vitamins A, D, E, and K from food. This can lead to problems with blood clotting and other functions like building muscles and bone.

## Serious Complications

When hepatitis progresses to cirrhosis, this can further impact liver function and lead to serious complications. Cirrhosis can slow blood circulation through the liver and cause blood to back up in the portal vein and in veins in the stomach, esophagus, and spleen. This can increase blood pressure, and these blood vessels may burst and bleed. If this occurs in the stomach and esophagus, it is called gastric and esophageal varices, and it can be life-threatening. When blood backs up into the spleen, this organ often becomes enlarged and traps the blood cells it manufactures. If the red blood cells cannot get out, it can lead to anemia (a shortage of red blood cells). A shortage of blood cells called platelets, which are needed for blood clotting, can lead to clotting disorders.

Another complication of cirrhosis is ascites, or fluid buildup in the abdomen. This is especially common in people with alcoholic hepatitis. A lack of albumin and kidney damage from a diseased liver can contribute to ascites, and the condition can be painful and even impact the ability to breathe. The fluid can also become infected.

Patients with the complications of ascites, hepatic encephalopathy, jaundice, and blood that cannot clot often develop life-threatening fulminant hepatitis or end-stage liver disease.

## Diagnosing Hepatitis

Since many symptoms and complications of hepatitis can also be characteristic of other liver diseases or of cancer or flu, a doctor cannot diagnose hepatitis based on symptoms alone. The physician must take a medical history, perform a physical exam, and conduct certain tests to ascertain whether the patient has hepatitis, and, if so, what type of hepatitis. The medical history involves asking questions about general health, diet, medication use, alcohol consumption, sexual activities, travel, exposure to toxins, and other habits. The physical exam may not reveal that anything is wrong with the liver, but sometimes the liver will feel enlarged from inflammation or abnormally hard from cirrhosis.

Routine blood tests can better indicate that something is wrong with the liver. For example, a prothrombin time (PT)

A technician prepares whole blood serum for hepatitis testing with radioimmunoassay, a method for detecting small amounts of antigens in blood.

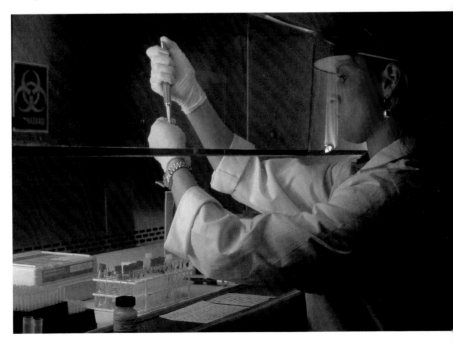

test, which measures how quickly blood clots, can reveal that the blood is not clotting normally. Blood tests for bilirubin, alkaline phosphatase, albumin, alpha-feta protein, and liver enzymes (proteins that regulate chemical reactions) such as aspartate aminotransferase (AST) and alanine aminotransferase (ALT) can give further clues that liver disease is present, but they cannot tell the doctor exactly what is wrong. AST and ALT levels are especially helpful in assessing the presence of liver disease, since a poorly functioning liver releases high levels of these enzymes into the blood. Tests for ALT and AST are often known as liver function tests.

In order to diagnose specific types of hepatitis and to assess the extent of liver damage, additional tests are necessary. Generally, a primary care physician will refer a patient to a gastroenterologist (specialist in digestive diseases) or a hepatologist (gastroenterologist who specializes in the liver) for these tests.

Hepatitis serology tests are blood tests used to determine which form of viral hepatitis a patient has. These tests measure specific antigens, or proteins found in the virus, and antibodies the body makes against these antigens. In addition, viral load tests can be conducted; these measure the amount of a particular virus in the blood. For example, doctors consider an individual with more than two million copies of the hepatitis C virus per milliliter of blood to have a high viral load. Viral load can help the physician predict how well a patient will respond to treatment and can be used to track treatment success. However, it does not tell the doctor how damaged the liver is; in fact, for reasons that are not yet understood, someone with a high viral load is less likely to have severe damage than is someone with a low viral load.

In diagnosing nonviral hepatitis, doctors perform blood tests for antinuclear antibodies, smooth muscle antibodies, and antibodies to liver and kidney microsomes when they suspect autoimmune hepatitis. These are all autoantibodies (antibodies that target the individual's own body) that can indicate the presence and subtype of AIH.

A doctor places a sample of liver tissue into a sterile box to be sent for analysis. A biopsy is a sample of living tissue that is analyzed in order to diagnose a medical condition.

There are no direct blood tests for toxic or alcoholic hepatitis or for nonalcoholic steatohepatitis, but blood tests that measure blood alcohol, drug, or toxin levels can be useful in diagnosing these disorders. Performing a liver biopsy can also help determine the type of hepatitis, and this procedure is considered the "gold standard" for assessing liver damage. Most doctors order a biopsy, which involves using a hollow needle to remove a small piece of the liver and examining the sample under a microscope, after they have diagnosed hepatitis, but it can also be helpful in determining whether someone has fatty liver–induced or alcoholic hepatitis. The biopsy can reveal fat deposits and can distinguish differences in the liver inflammation found in alcoholic versus viral hepatitis.

The main purpose of a liver biopsy is to quantify the extent of liver damage and inflammation. There are several staging and grading systems that physicians use to do this. The Knodell score, for example, rates the amount of scar tissue on a scale of zero to eighteen to determine the stage of liver damage and uses a scale of zero to four to indicate the amount, or grade, of inflammation. The Metavir system, on the other hand, uses four-point scales to rate both the stage and grade.

Once a physician has determined the type and severity of hepatitis that a patient has, he or she can make recommendations about treatment options and, in the case of contagious forms of the disease, about steps the person can take to prevent spreading the virus to others.

# Causes and Risk Factors

The various types of hepatitis reflect the diverse causes of the disease. Each type has a different cause and different risk factors. Risk factors are biological, environmental, or lifestyle characteristics that increase an individual's chances of being exposed to certain causes and developing a disease.

## Causes of Viral Hepatitis

Hepatitis viruses A, B, C, D, or E cause viral hepatitis. Viruses are submicroscopic organisms that can only be seen with an electron microscope. Scientists measure their size in nanometers; a nanometer is one billionth of a meter. Different viruses range in size from about fifteen to twenty-five nanometers. As a comparison, red blood cells are about 750 nanometers long.

Viruses are made primarily of DNA (deoxyribonucleic acid) or RNA (ribonucleic acid), which are the fundamental building blocks and instruction codes for all life forms. DNA and RNA molecules consist of a series of chemicals called bases or nucleotides. DNA usually consists of two long, intertwined strands of nucleotides, while RNA is made of one shorter strand. DNA strands function mainly as a set of blueprints that tell cells how to operate and produce chemicals. RNA serves mainly to translate these instructions so cells can read them.

Viral DNA or RNA is surrounded by an outer shell known as a capsid protein. Some viruses also have another layer inside the capsid called an envelope. Scientists classify viruses into

31

# The Discovery of the Hepatitis B Virus

The hepatitis B virus was the first hepatitis virus to be identified. Baruch Blumberg and his colleagues at Fox Chase Cancer Center in Philadelphia accidentally discovered the virus in 1967 while studying how genes influence susceptibility to diseases. The researchers traveled around the world collecting blood samples from people in diverse cultures. While analyzing blood taken from people with a clotting disorder called hemophilia, they discovered an antibody that matched an unknown antigen they had earlier found in the blood of an Australian native. Blumberg called the antigen "the Australia antigen." Intrigued by these discoveries, Blumberg and his team used electron microscopes and other molecular biology technologies to study the Australia antigen and to link it to a liver disease. They then analyzed thousands of patient blood samples and proved that the antigen was the virus that caused hepatitis B.

Blumberg received the Nobel Prize in Medicine in 1976 for the discovery, which experts have hailed as one of the greatest medical achievements of the twentieth century. He went on to develop a blood test to diagnose the virus and also invented the first hepatitis B vaccine in 1969.

The 1976 Nobel Laureate in medicine Baruch Blumberg, 1976. His prize-winning work, with D. Carleton Gajdusek, concerned the origin and dissemination of infectious diseases.

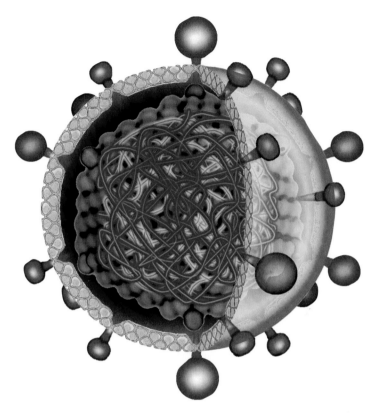

Hepatitis B Virus. Membrane (in yellow) with proteins (grey spheres), capsid (in grey), negative DNA strand (in blue), and positive DNA strand (in yellow).

families based on their size, shape, presence or absence of an envelope, and type of genome (genetic material—either DNA or RNA).

Viruses cannot live on their own. They require a host animal or plant to survive and must get inside a living cell to reproduce. Some viruses invade only certain types of cells. The viruses that cause hepatitis enter, or infect, only liver cells, and small as they are, they can do a great deal of damage.

When a virus infects a cell, it sheds its protein cover and uses the cell's machinery to replicate and assemble copies of its own genetic parts. These new viruses leave the cell and infect other cells. "The main goal of the hepatitis virus is to enter a liver cell,

# Causes of Hepatitis C in Celebrities With the Disease

Many celebrities with hepatitis C have brought attention to the causes of the disease.

- Actress Pamela Anderson contracted HCV from sharing an infected tattoo needle with ex-husband Tommy Lee.

- Country singer Naomi Judd was infected through an accidental needle stick that spread an infected patient's blood to her while she was working as a nurse.

- Chuck Negron, former lead singer of the band Three Dog Night, contracted the disease through illegal drug use.

- Phil Lesh, founder of the 1960's rock band The Grateful Dead, got HCV from illegal drug use.

- Steven Tyler, lead singer of the band Aerosmith, was infected through illegal drug use.

- Ken Kesey, author of *One Flew Over the Cuckoo's Nest,* got HCV through illegal drug use.

- Professional baseball player Mickey Mantle got HCV from a blood transfusion.

- Daredevil Evil Knievel became infected from a blood transfusion after one of his many motorcycle crashes.

- "Right to die" doctor Jack Kevorkian got HCV from performing blood transfusions during the Vietnam War.

- British fashion designer and socialite Serena Bute got HCV from drug use and needle sharing in the 1970s and unknowingly passed the disease to daughter Jazzy de Lisser when Jazzy was born in 1991.

reproduce more hepatitis viruses, destroy the cell, and move on to attack the next cell,"[10] explains liver expert Melissa Palmer.

The host animal produces antibodies and other immune chemicals and cells in response to a viral infection to try to kill the viruses. Eventually, the body gets rid of the infection or the virus overpowers the immune system and keeps replicating. This often occurs when the virus mutates to become resistant to the antibodies, and this can result in chronic infection or even death. In addition, some viruses, such as HBV and HCV, can hide in cells for many years without triggering an immune response or symptoms of infection, but symptoms can begin at any time if the damage caused by the virus becomes widespread.

Many viruses, like the hepatitis viruses, can be transmitted to other people—that is, they are contagious. Different hepatitis viruses are transmitted in different ways, some through the digestive system and others through bodily fluids.

## Hepatitis A and E

Although they are caused by different viruses, hepatitis A and E are spread in the same manner. HAV is an RNA virus in the family Picornaviridae and HEV is an RNA virus in the Caliciviridae family. People contract them by ingesting infected feces, usually tiny amounts, through the mouth. The viruses migrate to the liver, where they replicate and then are shed in feces. The viruses are contagious whether or not the infected person has symptoms and can survive outside the body for several months and infect others.

HEV is rarely seen in the United States but is common in countries with poor sanitation, where people often become infected by ingesting food (particularly shellfish) or water contaminated by sewage. People who live in crowded quarters or in refugee camps after disasters are at especially high risk of contracting HEV.

HAV occurs frequently in the United States as well as elsewhere in the world. "Most infections result from close personal contact with an infected household member or sex partner,"[11]

Hepatitis A infection often results from a person's contact with infected objects, then putting hands in mouth, or eating with their hands without washing them first.

says the CDC. Many infections also result from touching an infected object and putting the fingers in the mouth, or from eating or drinking contaminated food or water. Infected food handlers in homes, institutions, or restaurants often spread HAV when they touch food after using the bathroom and not washing their hands. Another common mode of infection is in day-care centers where caregivers are not careful about washing their hands after changing diapers and where toddlers often do not wash their hands after using the bathroom. Infections often occur in care centers for the mentally disabled for similar reasons.

Anyone can get HAV, but in the United States those at highest risk for contracting and spreading it are men who have sex with other men, illegal drug users, people with other liver diseases, people who work with nonhuman primates that carry HAV, international travelers, and immigrants from countries with poor sanitation and hygiene. In some developing countries, more than 90 percent of the population has had HAV at some point, often from ingesting food or water that is contaminated with sewage. Sometimes poor sanitation practices like dumping sewage into rivers can even spread HAV to areas that usually have good sanitation. For example, on many occasions, health officials in San Diego have had to close Imperial Beach near the Mexican border because huge amounts of HAV-infected sewage from the Tijuana River flowed into the Pacific Ocean and sickened swimmers and surfers.

## Hepatitis B and D

HBV is a DNA virus in the family Hepadnaviridae. When the liver becomes infected with HBV, the virus also gets into the blood and other body fluids like saliva, semen, and vaginal secretions, and it is spread through contact with these fluids. HBV can enter the body through open sores, needle punctures, blood vessels, sexual organs, and the eyes, nose, or mouth.

In the United States, "Sexual contact is the most common means of transmission. The majority of reported acute HBV infections are among adolescents and young adults,"[12] explains Hepatitis Foundation International. Other common ways HBV is spread is by sharing needles and other illegal drug supplies; sharing razors or toothbrushes that have small amounts of blood on them; the use of infected tattooing, body piercing, and dental supplies; infected mothers passing the virus to a baby at birth; people on kidney dialysis exposed to infected blood through dialysis machines and intravenous tubing; and health care workers exposed to blood through accidental needle sticks.

People at highest risk are homosexuals, those with multiple sex partners, those with other sexually transmitted diseases, travelers to areas where HBV is prevalent, and illegal drug users. In addition, prisoners are at very high risk. According to the CDC, "Adults in correctional facilities are at risk for Hepatitis B virus (HBV) infection through sex with HBV-infected persons, injection drug use, and sharing close living quarters with other inmates infected with HBV. In addition, a high percentage of prison inmates have Hepatitis C (HCV) infection."[13]

The most common modes of infection in developing countries are infected mothers passing the virus to a baby, children infecting other children through cuts and bites, blood transfusions, and sexual contact. Blood transfusions and organ transplants used to be a primary mode of transmission in the United States too, but nowadays donated blood and organs are screened for hepatitis viruses, and laws prohibit people at high risk from donating. Rarely, the screening tests do not detect the viruses, so there is still a slight chance of becoming infected in this manner.

Hepatitis D virus is an RNA virus in the Deltaviridae family. It is what is known as an incomplete virus; that is, it needs

The most common mode of infection of hepatitis B in developing countries is the passing of the virus from mother to child.

another virus to replicate. The other virus it needs is HBV. That is why only people infected with HBV can get HDV. Like HBV, HDV is spread through infected body fluids, and people can contract it either at the same time as they get HBV or later on. Those at highest risk are individuals with multiple sex partners and illegal drug users.

## Hepatitis C

HCV is an RNA virus in the family Flaviviridae. It is usually spread through contact with infected blood. It can also be transmitted sexually, but, unlike with HBV, this does not happen often. The most common cause of HCV in the United States is sharing contaminated drug syringes or tattoo or body piercing needles. More than 30 percent of illegal injection drug users ages eighteen to thirty and 70–90 percent of older and former injection drug users have HCV, even if they only injected drugs once. "The high HCV prevalence among former IDUinjection drug users is largely attributable to needle sharing during the 1970's and 1980's, before the risks of bloodborne viruses were widely known and before educational initiatives were implemented,"[14] explains the CDC.

But even though many people are now aware of the dangers, they still engage in high-risk behaviors. Jake, for example, explains how he contracted HCV in 2005.

> During my last relationship my partner and I started occasionally using methamphetamine (meth) and practiced group sex while occasionally throwing caution to the wind... One weekend things got out of control and I injected meth with a shared needle... A few days later I got quite frightened and went to my MD for a blood test. Soon thereafter my worst fears were realized in that I found out I had hepatitis C.[15]

HCV is also commonly spread through infected kidney dialysis machines, from infected mothers to their newborns, through sharing infected razors or toothbrushes, or from

Hepatitis C is believed to be transmitted only by blood. However, unlike many other blood borne viruses (like HIV), virtually any source of blood or blood products seems to be capable of carrying the virus, even if the source is indirect—like a used razor, for example.

infected patients to health care workers. The virus can live for up to four days outside the body on surfaces and for a week or more inside syringes. Debbie, a nurse, explains how she was infected: "I recently was hit in the face by an object thrown by a physician. It was covered in blood, therefore I got a patient's blood in my eyes, nose, and mouth. The hospital refused to test me to start with but with my insistence and a letter from my attorney they agreed. I am Hep C positive."[16]

People who received blood clotting factor medicines before 1987, when safety standards were implemented, or blood transfusions or organ transplants before 1992, when screening for HCV began, are also at high risk. In developing countries, these modes of infection, as well as the use of unsterilized medical equipment, are still common.

## Autoimmune Hepatitis

The causes of AIH are not as well understood as are the causes of viral hepatitis, but researchers believe that a combination of genetic and environmental factors are involved. Scientists have found that some people are genetically susceptible to autoimmune diseases, but that environmental or biological triggers like poisons, viruses, or drugs are also needed for such individuals to actually develop the disorder.

A genetic predisposition, or susceptibility, is different than a direct transmission of inherited traits. Genes, which are the parts of a DNA molecule that pass hereditary information from parents to their children, appear in sequences on wormlike bodies called chromosomes in the center of each cell. The precise sequence of genes encodes a set of instructions telling the cell what to do. These instructions can be passed directly, as in the case of traits like hair color or eye color, and appear in the offspring at birth regardless of biological or environmental events. Or, the codes may be transmitted as an inherited tendency that requires additional factors to be realized.

Scientists are not sure about which genes are responsible for imparting a predisposition to AIH, but they are studying many likely candidates. They are also studying how and why certain viruses and drugs seem to trigger the disorder. Viruses associated with AIH include hepatitis A, B, and C; measles virus; and Epstein-Barr virus, which causes mononucleosis. Drugs linked to AIH are interferon, melatonin, alpha methyldopa, oxyphenisatin, nitrofurantoin, and tienilic acid. These triggers seem to be capable of causing AIH both shortly after exposure or a long time later. Whatever the underlying trigger for the autoimmune attack on liver cells may be, this attack ultimately causes AIH by inflaming and damaging these cells.

## Toxic Hepatitis

Some people may also have a genetic predisposition to develop toxic hepatitis, which explains why not everyone who is exposed to certain poisons or drugs linked to liver damage will end up with the disease. Females, whose livers tend to break down toxins more slowly than those of males, and people with genetic defects that lead to deficiencies in liver enzymes that break down drugs, are most likely to develop toxic hepatitis after exposure to poisons or after ingesting certain drugs. People in some racial groups are also more prone to liver inflammation from certain drugs. African Americans and Hispanics,

Seniors are more likely to contract toxic hepatitis as their livers break down toxins more slowly.

for example, are more likely than Caucasians to experience liver toxicity from isoniazid, used to treat tuberculosis.

Risk factors other than genetics can affect the likelihood of toxic hepatitis as well. Older adults are at high risk because their livers break down toxins more slowly than happens in younger people, and these poisons thus remain in the body longer. People with other liver diseases like fatty liver or viral hepatitis also cannot process toxins and drugs properly and must be very careful about ingesting even normal doses of many medications. Individuals who are constantly exposed to industrial toxins on the job are also at high risk. One study of a group of workers at an industrial waste plant revealed that exposure to the chemicals pyridine, dimethylformamide, dimethylacetamide, and methylenedianiline caused many cases of toxic hepatitis.

When the liver breaks down drugs or toxins, it can be damaged by the substances themselves or by the by-products of their breakdown. Some toxins directly kill liver cells, while others interfere with the cells' metabolism or energy production. Many cases of toxic hepatitis are caused by drugs that bind to the P-450 enzyme that detoxifies them. When this binding occurs, for some reason the immune system responds by sending out chemicals that cause inflammation.

## Toxins That Cause Hepatitis

Experts divide toxins that cause liver damage into two groups. One group includes poisons that always cause liver damage by overwhelming the liver so it cannot process them. Examples are dry cleaning solvents, industrial chemicals like trichloroethylene, herbicides like paraquat, and deathcap mushrooms. If the damage is severe enough, liver failure results. The second group includes toxins that may or may not cause liver damage, depending on the amount and on the individual. Many prescription and nonprescription drugs and herbal supplements fall into this category. Acetaminophen, a drug found in many painkillers, causes many cases of toxic hepatitis when people take more than the recommended amount or use alcohol at the same time. Other pain medicines like aspirin and ibuprofen are also associated with many instances of the disease. The tuberculosis drug isoniazid is likely to cause toxic hepatitis from normal doses, and many people avoid it for this reason. Many cancer drugs like methotrexate, antibiotics like trovfloxacin, and antifungal drugs like ketoconazole also frequently lead to liver damage soon after they are started, and doctors try to avoid using these drugs in at-risk patients.

The Food and Drug Administration (FDA) has withdrawn many drugs from the market because they caused hepatitis in many people. These include the pain medicine bromfenac, the diabetes drug troglitazone, and the attention deficit disorder drug pemoline. The FDA also requires drug manufacturers to place liver toxicity warnings on many drugs.

Although many people believe that herbal supplements are healthy and safe, experts caution that some can cause toxic hepatitis. "The fact that herbs are natural preparations from plants doesn't necessarily mean they are safe,"[17] says Hepatitis Foundation International. Herbs and other dietary supplements are not regulated by the FDA as drugs are, and marketers frequently make false and misleading claims about their healing powers. Herbs that are proven to seriously harm the liver include chaparral, Jin Bu Huan, germander, comfrey, mistletoe, skullcap, margosa oil, mate tea, Gordolobo yerba tea, and pennyroyal. In one case, a woman who took chaparral tablets, which are touted for their anticancer and blood purifying effects, developed severe toxic hepatitis and needed a liver transplant.

## Alcoholic Hepatitis

In a manner similar to that seen in toxic hepatitis, alcohol causes hepatitis when the liver breaks it down into toxic chemicals, particularly acetaldehyde, which inflames and kills liver cells. Alcohol also causes fat to build up in the liver, and this fat can inflame liver cells. Scientists believe that the immune system also plays a role in causing alcoholic hepatitis. The immune system launches white blood cells to fight the chemicals found in alcohol, and this further inflames the liver. This immune response may help explain why the inflammation in alcoholic hepatitis can last well beyond the time the patient stops drinking.

Anyone who consumes alcohol is at risk for alcoholic hepatitis, but it is most likely to occur in people who drink heavily over many years. Females, who often have fewer enzymes that break down alcohol than males do; individuals who have gene mutations that

Alcoholic hepatitis is liver inflammation caused by drinking excessive amounts of alcohol.

affect alcohol metabolism; and people who are malnourished are at particular risk of developing the disease even if they do not consume a lot of alcohol.

## Nonalcoholic Steatohepatitis

When excess fat is stored in hepatocytes in people who do not drink alcohol, this can inflame the cells and cause NASH. The nonalcoholic fatty liver disease (NAFLD) that is responsible for NASH is usually caused by a combination of health problems called metabolic syndrome. Metabolic syndrome includes obesity (especially belly fat), high blood pressure, and insulin resistance or type 2 diabetes. Insulin is a hormone made in the pancreas that pushes glucose into cells and prevents blood sugar levels from becoming too high. People with type 2 diabetes may not produce enough insulin, or their cells may be resistant to insulin. Cells in people with insulin resistance have faulty insulin receptors that do not allow insulin to work properly. Glucose builds up in the blood, so the body produces more insulin to try to reduce the blood sugar level. But when insulin cannot be used, it too accumulates in the bloodstream, and this leads to fat buildup as well. The fat gets deposited in the liver, and NAFLD results.

However, some people with NAFLD and NASH do not have any or all of the components of metabolic syndrome. "Some patients with NASH are not obese, do not have diabetes, and have normal blood cholesterol and lipidsfats. NASH can occur without any apparent risk factors and can even occur in children. Thus, NASH is not simply obesity that affects the liver,"[18] explains NIDDK.

Since so many people are at risk for developing NASH, as well as other types of hepatitis, public health officials have made educating people about the known risks a priority in hopes of preventing many cases of the disease.

# CHAPTER THREE

# Prevention

**P**ublic health agencies and nonprofit advocacy groups emphasize that prevention is much preferable to treatment; thus they are striving to get the word out to health care professionals and the public about methods of preventing the various types of hepatitis. There are different ways of preventing each type, and the CDC has taken the lead in issuing reports outlining prevention strategies, particularly for viral hepatitis. They publish guidelines for health care and social service professionals, tips for the public, and special traveler advisories for people who travel to areas of the world where hepatitis is rampant. CDC also keeps track of cases of hepatitis in the United States (doctors are required to report cases to public health departments) to assess how well preventive measures are working.

One important weapon in the prevention of viral hepatitis is vaccines, which consist of inactivated viruses that stimulate the immune system to produce antibodies. The vaccinated individual becomes immune to being infected by the virus. At the present time, vaccines are available to prevent hepatitis A and B, and researchers are busy developing vaccines for other forms of viral hepatitis.

## Preventing Hepatitis A and E

Vaccines for HAV have been available since Maurice Hilleman developed the first HAV vaccine in 1995. Scientists make the vaccine by growing the virus in a cell culture and killing it with a poison called formalin. There are three HAV vaccines licensed for use in the United States: HAVRIX, VAQTA, and TWINRIX (a combination HAV and HBV vaccine). They are given by injection and provide protection from HAV for at least twenty-five years in adults and at least fourteen to twenty years in children. the CDC recommends that anyone with risk factors for HAV receive the vaccine and that all one-year-old children get it as well.

The CDC says the vaccine has improved prevention of HAV significantly: "Hepatitis A rates in the United States have declined by 92% since Hepatitis A vaccine first became available in 1995."[19] However, vaccination does not occur nearly as frequently elsewhere in the world, particularly in developing countries, and the number of infections has not declined nearly as much in these places.

Unvaccinated people who have been exposed to HAV can often prevent illness by getting a vaccination or receiving an immunoglobulin (IG) injection within two weeks. IG is made of concentrated antibodies and provides protection from infection for about three months. Doctors often give IG to patients such as infants under age one, who are too young to receive HAV vaccine; older people who may not respond to the vaccine; and anyone with chronic liver disease, allergies to components of the vaccine, or diseases that weaken the immune system and make getting a vaccine dangerous.

Other methods of preventing HAV infection include "avoiding tap water when traveling internationally and practicing good hygiene and sanitation,"[20] says NIDDK. People can also add chlorine to water or boil it, avoid eating uncooked or unpeeled shellfish, fruits, and vegetables, and heat foods to 185 degrees Fahrenheit for one minute to kill HAV when they travel to areas where it is common.

Preventing HEV is achieved in the same manner as for HAV, except that there is currently no approved HEV vaccine, and immunoglobulin injections do not work either. Drug companies make IG from antibodies obtained from the blood of infected donors, and for some reason, this blood rarely contains enough HEV antibodies to make an effective IG solution. Scientists are, however, working on developing an effective vaccine. In fact,

# Dr. Maurice Hilleman

Microbiologist Maurice Hilleman developed the first hepatitis A vaccine in 1995, and it has prevented millions of cases of the disease since that time. Hilleman was born in 1919 and grew up on a farm in Montana. His family was poor, and he never expected to go to college, but he received a scholarship and graduated from Montana State University in 1941. He then earned his PhD in microbiology from the University of Chicago.

After working for drug manufacturer E.R. Squibb and for the Walter Reed Army Hospital, he joined Merck Pharmaceuticals in 1957 to direct a virus research program. While at Merck, he developed many animal vaccines and human vaccines for mumps, measles, rubella, chicken pox, pneumonia, meningitis, and hepatitis B, as well as for HAV. In fact, he developed more vaccines than any other scientist in the world. In addition, he discovered several viruses, including hepatitis A virus, and made significant advances in understanding how viruses mutate. In 1988 President Ronald Reagan presented Hilleman with the National Medal of Science for saving countless lives and preventing millions of disabilities. Hilleman also received numerous other awards throughout the world.

He died in 2005 in Philadelphia and, despite his many achievements, remains virtually unknown except in scientific circles. His colleagues say this is because he shunned the limelight. In a tribute to Hilleman after his death, one colleague said, "Maurice was not someone disposed to taking personal credit for his achievements. He was always quick to give credit to his team members. It was never about him. Rather, the reward was in the products developed, the lives saved."

Anthony Fauci "Biographical Memoirs" *Proceedings of the American Philosophical Society* vol. 151, no. 4 (2007). www.niaid.nih.gov/about/directors/documents/hillemanessay.pdf.

Researcher Dr. Maurice Hilleman working in a lab at Walter Reed Research Institute studying the flu virus.

researchers in China tested one promising experimental vaccine known as HEV 239 on nearly 100,000 people and reported in August 2010 that it appears to work very well. No one given three doses of the vaccine over a six-month period contracted hepatitis E during the study, and even those who received only two doses within one month were well protected. The drug also seems to be safe in that it caused only mild side effects such as swelling and pain at the injection site. The investigators are planning further studies to assess long-term safety and effectiveness before the vaccine can be approved for widespread use.

## Preventing Hepatitis B and D

HDV can only be prevented by not becoming infected with HBV; there is no HDV vaccine. But there is an HBV vaccine, which scientists make by genetically engineering and inactivating the HBV virus. The vaccine is given in two, three, or four doses, depending on the brand used, and provides protection for at least fifteen years. Several teams of researchers are currently seeking to determine exactly how long after vaccination immunity to HBV lasts, so public health officials can make recommendations on whether booster shots are needed. One study by drug manufacturer GlaxoSmithKline, for example, is measuring blood antibody levels of both HAV and HBV sixteen, seventeen, eighteen, nineteen, and twenty years after vaccination with the combination TWINRIX vaccine to assess when antibody levels start to decline.

HBV vaccines have been available since 1981 and have done much to curtail the spread of the virus, especially since widespread immunizations began in 1991 in many countries. The CDC says the rate of new HBV infections has declined by about 82 percent since 1991 in the United States. Many doctors have also hailed the HBV vaccine as the first anticancer vaccine, since preventing HBV helps prevent many cases of liver cancer.

Currently, infants in the United States and in some other countries routinely receive the HBV vaccine at birth, but in

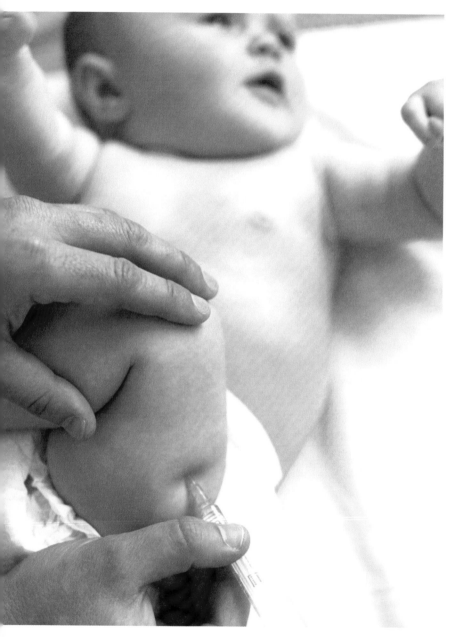

A four-month-old baby has a vaccine injected into her leg from a syringe. Vaccination provides long-term protection against infectious diseases. It is common for newborns to be vaccinated a day or two after birth in the hospital.

many developing countries it is not available or affordable. Public health officials in the United States also recommend vaccinations for adults at high risk and for children and adolescents who were not vaccinated at birth. Some school districts require the immunization before a child begins school.

The CDC and most health professionals say the HBV vaccine is safe, but controversy over its safety has led many people to refuse to be vaccinated or to allow their children to be vaccinated. Several studies have linked HBV vaccine to an unusually high number of cases of type 1 diabetes and multiple sclerosis (MS), which are both serious autoimmune diseases. In type 1 diabetes, the body destroys the insulin-producing cells in the pancreas, and in MS it attacks nerve cells in the brain and spinal cord. In 1998 the French Ministry of Health banned routine HBV immunizations of school-aged children because of these findings, but they continued to recommend vaccinations for infants because the risk of developing diabetes or MS seemed to be lower for babies. The Ministry later rescinded the ban and resumed immunizations for children and adolescents when subsequent studies failed to demonstrate that HBV vaccine actually caused diabetes and MS.

Later studies, though, have continued to inflame the safety debate. One British study reported in 2004 in the journal *Neurology*, for example, found that people who received the HBV vaccine were three times more likely to develop MS than those who did not receive it. A 2008 study reported in *The Open Pediatric Medicine Journal* found that the vaccine significantly increased the risk of type 1 diabetes in children in Italy, France, and New Zealand. "Data from Italy, France, and New Zealand indicated rises in the incidence of IDDM insulin-dependent diabetes mellitus occurred between 24 to 48 months after the introduction of the hepatitis B immunization in young children,"[21] explained the doctor who conducted the study.

But most studies have not found a link between HBV vaccine and diabetes or MS, and public health agencies continue to advocate widespread vaccinations for people of all ages. In a statement about the vaccine and MS, for instance, the

# How People With Hepatitis B Can Prevent Spreading the Disease

Hepatitis Foundation International says it is important for people already infected with viral hepatitis to prevent spreading it to others. Their suggestions for preventing the spread of HBV include:

- Wash your hands with soap after touching your own blood or body fluids. Throw personal items such as tissues, menstrual pads, tampons, or bandages away in a plastic bag.

- All cuts and sores should be covered with a bandage. Wipe up your blood spills, then reclean the area with a solution of one part household bleach to ten parts water.

- Tell sexual partners you have hepatitis B. Partners should be tested for HBV, and if not immune to the virus, they should receive the vaccination series of three shots. Until protection from HBV has been guaranteed, use a condom.

- Do not share food that has been in your mouth and do not pre-chew food for babies.

- Do not donate blood, plasma, body organs, tissue, or sperm.

Hepatitis Foundation International. "Living With Hepatitis." www.hepfi.org/living/liv_living.html.

CDC stated, "The weight of the available evidence does not support the suggestion that hepatitis B vaccine causes or worsens MS."[22]

Besides receiving the HBV vaccine, people can also prevent infection by getting a hepatitis B immunoglobulin injection within twenty-four hours after exposure to the virus. But many people do not know they have been exposed and thus do not get the immunoglobulin, so experts say it is better to take the vaccine, which provides long-term protection.

## Preventing Hepatitis C

There is currently no vaccine for HCV, but scientists are working on developing one. The task is especially challenging because HCV mutates rapidly, and the immune system cannot keep responding to changes in the virus. Drug manufacturer Okairos in England recently developed a new HCV vaccine they believe may surmount these challenges, and they are currently running tests on a small group of patients who already have HCV to see if the vaccine promotes an immune response to the virus. If it does, tests on uninfected people may proceed.

Doctors say that until a vaccine is approved, the best way of preventing HCV (and HBV, for those who have not been vaccinated) is by using latex condoms, not sharing drug needles or other drug tools, not sharing items like razors or toothbrushes, and not getting tattoos or body piercings in businesses that reuse needles.

The CDC has also published a "National Hepatitis B and C Prevention Strategy" that offers advice on preventing HBV and HCV to health care professionals and the public. For example, the strategy recommends that all pregnant women be screened for HBV and that all babies born to infected women receive immediate injections of hepatitis B immunoglobulin and vaccine after birth. It provides guidelines for educating hospital and clinic workers about preventing HBV and HCV by wearing gowns, gloves, and masks if necessary, and instructs kidney dialysis centers on effective methods of sterilizing or disposing of equipment and supplies to reduce the risks to patients. The report also advises medical and law enforcement personnel to clean any blood spills in or outside of hospitals with a solution of one part bleach to ten parts water, and encourages clinics that provide services for sexually transmitted diseases to routinely administer HBV vaccinations.

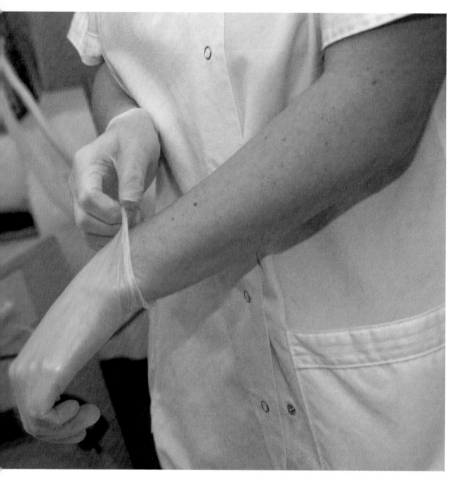

The CDC recommends all hospital and clinic workers wear protective clothing, such as gloves and masks, to help prevent the spread of hepatitis C.

## Preventing Autoimmune Hepatitis

There is no conclusive research on methods of preventing AIH, but some scientists have suggested that preventing infections with viruses associated with triggering AIH and avoiding drugs linked to the disease may help. For example, HAV and HBV may trigger AIH, so getting vaccinated against these viruses may help prevent AIH. Avoiding drugs like interferon, methyldopa, and nitrofurantoin if other drugs are available to treat an underlying disease may also prove to be an effective way of reducing the risk of AIH.

## Preventing Alcoholic Hepatitis

Doctors say that preventing alcoholic hepatitis is simple: Don't drink alcohol, or drink only in moderation. Experts define moderation as no more than one drink per day for women and no more than two per day for men. However, "The only certain way to prevent alcoholic hepatitis is to avoid all alcohol,"[23] say doctors at the Mayo Clinic, since even moderate drinkers can get the disease.

## Preventing Nonalcoholic Steatohepatitis

Although most people who get NASH are obese, this is not always true, so preventing obesity is not a fail-proof way of preventing NASH. But doctors say that many cases of NASH can be prevented by following a low-fat diet, getting regular exercise, and losing weight gradually if weight loss is needed, particularly if the excess weight is in the belly and if the individual has NAFLD. Howard J. Worman, author of *The Liver Disorders and Hepatitis Sourcebook*, sums it up by saying, "Obese patients with fatty liver who lead unhealthy lifestyles should consider fatty liver a warning sign for development of other serious diseases. They should heed this warning and start leading healthier lives."[24] Avoiding alcohol, drugs, and herb supplements that can damage the liver can also help prevent NAFLD from progressing to NASH because these substances promote liver inflammation.

## Preventing Toxic Hepatitis

Sometimes toxic hepatitis results from normal use of medications, and in these cases it cannot be prevented. But many times taking too much medicine causes the disease, so following drug packaging and doctors' directions and not exceeding the recommended dosage can help prevent it. Being careful about not using multiple drugs that together can adversely affect the liver, not mixing alcohol and drugs, not taking herbs that can

Mixing medication and alcohol can cause toxic hepatitis.

damage the liver, preventing children from having access to drugs and poisons, and not using harmful substances like solvents, pesticides, and herbicides in the home or workplace can also help prevent toxic hepatitis.

When prevention of any type of hepatitis fails and infection occurs, the next step is treatment. But treatments are not available for all types of hepatitis, and even when available they are not always effective.

# CHAPTER FOUR

# Treatment

**L**ike prevention, hepatitis treatment depends on the type and duration of the disease. Treatment for acute hepatitis usually involves plenty of rest, fluids, and good nutrition. There are no drugs to specifically treat acute hepatitis, though medications can be given to relieve fever or pain. If the patient cannot eat or drink or develops fulminant hepatitis, he or she may have to be hospitalized to receive intravenous fluids and other live-saving therapy.

According to the author of *The Liver Disorders and Hepatitis Sourcebook*, "The therapeutic goal in acute liver disease is to keep the patient alive and, in some cases, to prevent the disease from becoming chronic. This involves supporting the patient until it spontaneously resolves."[25]

Several studies have suggested that the drug alpha interferon, which is used to treat chronic HBV and HCV, can be effective in keeping acute HCV from becoming chronic, but doctors point out that this has limited potential because most people with acute HCV do not know they are infected.

## Treating Chronic Viral Hepatitis

In contrast to the goals of treatment for acute hepatitis, "the therapeutic goal in chronic liver disease is to cure the disorder, prevent it from advancing, or control the complications."[26] At the present time, chronic HCV is the only form of chronic viral hepatitis that can be cured. HBV can often be controlled with medication, but cannot be cured because it is a DNA virus which enters the host DNA and becomes part of it. In contrast,

HCV is an RNA virus that does not get stuck in the host DNA, so it can be eradicated.

Not everyone with chronic viral hepatitis, however, needs or can benefit from drug treatment. Doctors decide who should be treated based on blood test and liver biopsy results and on other health problems the patient may have. A physician will perform blood tests to determine whether the virus is actively replicating or dormant. "It is important to emphasize that all of the available drugs really only work when there is evidence of active viral replication,"[27] explains the author of *The Liver Disorders and Hepatitis Sourcebook*. In addition, people with serious complications of cirrhosis or those who have diabetes, thyroid disorders, anemia, or clotting problems are generally not good candidates for drug treatment because the drugs' side effects can worsen these disorders.

## Hepatitis B Treatment

The goal of HBV treatment is to slow replication of the virus and thereby to stop or slow the progression of liver damage. Doctors prescribe antiviral drugs, which interfere with virus replication and strengthen the immune system for this purpose.

There were no effective treatments for chronic hepatitis prior to the invention of artificial interferon in the late 1970s, but today several different drugs are used. Interferon is a cytokine (chemical messenger) that occurs naturally in the immune system. It is important for helping the immune system recognize viruses and launch an attack against them. It also interferes with virus replication, prevents viruses from entering cells, and directly kills viruses. Many of the symptoms people experience when they become infected with a virus, such as fever and muscle pain, result from the interferon the body produces to fight off the virus.

The immune system makes three types of interferon: alpha, beta, and gamma. Each affects the immune system slightly differently. But the body only makes small amounts of these chemicals, so scientists figured out methods of using genetic engineering to make synthetic forms of each type to boost the immune system. Doctors use different types of synthetic interferon to treat different diseases. Alpha interferon is the type used to treat hepatitis. There is also a newer version of alpha interferon called pegylated or peginterferon. This version includes a molecule that makes it last longer in the body, so patients only have to inject it once a week, as opposed to three times a week for regular alpha interferon. Most HBV patients take alpha or peginterferon for forty-eight weeks. Of those, 40–60 percent respond favorably to treatment; their viral load diminishes or sometimes becomes undetectable, liver enzyme levels return to normal, and liver inflammation subsides. Another important

Newer versions of the hepatitis B treatment drug alpha interferon last longer in the body, so the patients only have to inject the drug once a week.

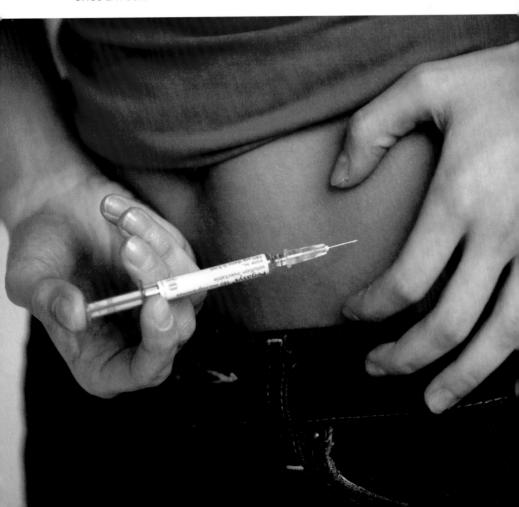

# The Discovery of Interferon

In 1954 Yasuhiko Kojima and Yasu-ichi Nagano at Tokyo University in Japan discovered a natural protein that made laboratory rabbits resistant to viruses. Then, in 1957, the Scottish virologist Alick Issacs and the Swiss scientist Jean Lindenmann found that this same protein destroyed viruses injected into chick embryos and inhibited the growth of other viruses. Issacs and Lindenmann named the protein interferon because it interfered with virus growth. Since they named the protein, Issacs and Lindenmann are often given sole credit for its discovery.

Subsequent research found that people and animals produce interferon within hours after a virus enters the body. Thus, it became known as the first line of defense against viruses. Other defensive mechanisms such as antibodies take longer to form.

Scientists also discovered three types of interferon: alpha, beta, and gamma, and began trying to make synthetic interferon to boost the body's immune response. In the late 1960s, American researcher Ion Gresser and Finnish scientist Kari Cantell discovered a method of extracting interferon from human blood cells and manufacturing small amounts of synthetic interferon from the extract. However, this synthetic was not pure, and it was not until the late 1970s that other scientists succeeded in purifying it so it could be used therapeutically.

In the mid-1980s, new genetic engineering techniques such as DNA cloning allowed scientists to produce enough artificial interferon to treat many patients with diseases such as HBV and HCV.

indicator of successful HBV treatment is whether a patient who was HBeAg positive becomes HBeAg negative. The presence of the HBeAg antigen in the blood shows the virus is active, whereas an HBeAg negative reading means it has become inactive. Patients who are HBeAg negative are much less likely to develop cirrhosis or liver failure.

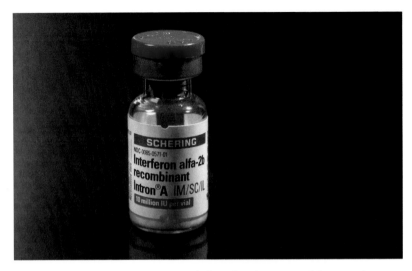

Interferon ALPHA-2B, an antiviral drug, has been used for a wide range of indications, including hepatitis B and C.

Even patients who respond well to treatment can experience a relapse, or recurrence of symptoms later on, since the HBV virus is not actually eradicated. For this reason, doctors recommend that anyone who has ever had HBV should have periodic blood tests to measure virus activity.

## Side Effects From Interferon

Interferon can have serious side effects, and some people stop taking it before completing treatment for this reason. Others cannot afford the drugs—they cost more than $30,000 per year—and must stop or never start the treatment for this reason as well, especially if they lack medical insurance.

Side effects may include fever, aches, mental confusion, nausea, vomiting, diarrhea, loss of appetite, depression, skin rashes, fatigue, weakness, and hair loss. Some patients become completely bedridden from severe side effects. Interferon can also damage bone marrow, where blood cells are produced, and blood cell deficiencies can result in death if they are serious enough. Doctors frequently monitor blood cell counts during treatment to prevent this from happening.

Some patients say the side effects of interferon are worse than the hepatitis itself. Dee, for example, was overwhelmed by some of the ill effects she experienced. "The first injection hit me about 5 hours later – and I mean hit! I felt like I had the worst case of the flu ever. I had fever and chills for several hours, and then the headache and body aches set in...By week three I had to have something for depression. I became anemic and by the end of it all lost 50 pounds. I lost a lot of my hair."[28]

Many people require treatment for these side effects. Some need psychotherapy and drugs for depression. Many need pain and antinausea medicines or drugs to build up their blood cell counts. But people with hepatitis must be very careful about taking any drugs because their livers cannot process the drugs efficiently, and doctors sometimes will not prescribe medicine for side effects because they fear this would overload the liver.

## Other Hepatitis B Treatments

Besides interferon, there are several other antiviral drugs used to treat HBV. These medications have the advantages that they can be taken by mouth rather than by injection and have fewer side effects. They are also less expensive than interferon; prices range from about $4,000 to $10,000 per year. However, they do not provide long-lasting results for as many patients as interferon does.

Lamivudine was the first oral antiviral medication to be approved for HBV treatment in the 1990s. It works by inhibiting an enzyme called DNA polymerase in the hepatitis B virus. Without this enzyme, the virus cannot replicate. However, nearly half of the people treated with lamivudine relapse after they stop taking it, and 60–70 percent of the time the virus mutates to become resistant to the drug after five years. Newer antivirals like adefovir, entecavir, telbivudine, and tenofovir do not induce viral mutations nearly as often as lamivudine does, but many patients relapse if they stop taking these drugs as well. Scientists are trying to find other drugs that provide longer-lasting results.

# Hepatitis C Treatment

Standard treatment for HCV involves interferon alpha or peginterferon injections combined with the oral antiviral drug ribavirin. Ribavirin boosts the effectiveness of interferon, but is not effective if used by itself. Even so, the combination of interferon and ribavirin is only successful in curing HCV about 50 percent of the time. Doctors define success in HCV treatment as having a sustained virologic response (SVR) for six months after treatment ends. An SVR means the virus is no

Hepatitis C treatments consist of ribavirin (antiviral drug) and injections of pegylated interferon.

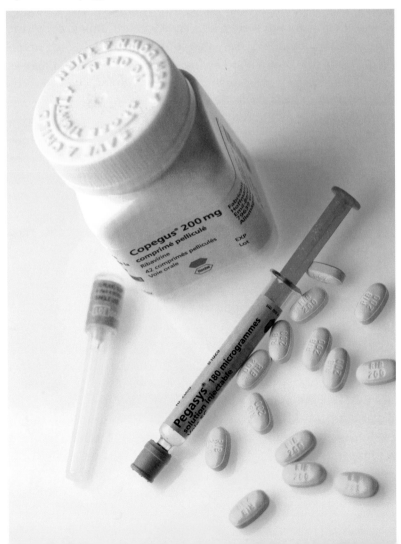

longer present in the blood. However, some patients who are not actually cured relapse after a SVR if the virus was undetectable but still present.

Those who do not have good results with standard treatment can try a type of interferon called consensus interferon. This drug is more potent than alpha interferon or peginterferon, but it does not last as long and must be injected daily. A 2006 study showed that consensus interferon plus ribavirin helped 20–25 percent of HCV patients who did not respond to peginterferon.

Like interferon, ribavirin can have serious side effects, including depression, heart problems, anemia, and birth defects if taken by pregnant women. For some patients, the combined side effects from interferon and ribavirin are unbearable. British socialite Jazzy de Lisser, also known as "The It Girl," experienced horrific pain, mood swings, hair loss, and mouth sores, and her treatment was unsuccessful anyway. "I wouldn't try this treatment again,"[29] she stated in a CNN interview.

The duration of HCV treatment depends on which genotype (genetic variation) of the virus a patient has. Scientists have identified six HCV genotypes and more than fifty subtypes. People with genotypes two and three generally respond well to twenty-four weeks of treatment. Those with genotype one are less likely to respond well, and doctors usually treat them for forty-eight weeks. However, some doctors find that tailoring treatment to each individual works better than following the standard recommendations. "My personal experience has been that some people require as little as six weeks of therapy, whereas others need as long as two to three years on continuous therapy to achieve viral eradication. Clearly, treatment needs to be approached on an individualized basis,"[30] says Melissa Palmer.

## Treatment for Autoimmune Hepatitis

Treatment for AIH involves drugs that suppress the immune system so it will stop attacking liver tissue. These drugs may include daily doses of corticosteroids like prednisone and another drug called azathioprine. Treatment may begin with high doses of prednisone that the doctor gradually lowers as the disease comes under control. Azathioprine allows patients to take lower doses of prednisone, so doctors often combine the two. It is important that patients take the lowest possible dose of prednisone because it has serious side effects such as infection, cancer, weight gain, confusion, anxiety, osteoporosis, diabetes, thinning hair and skin, high blood pressure, and cataracts. Azathioprine has fewer side effects; these may include nausea and low white blood cell counts.

AIH symptoms diminish or go away, liver enzyme levels improve, and liver inflammation decreases in about 70 percent of patients treated with these drugs. But AIH cannot be cured, and many patients must continue taking medication for the rest of their lives.

## Treatment for Alcoholic Hepatitis

The primary treatment for alcoholic hepatitis is consuming no alcohol. "If you're diagnosed with alcoholic hepatitis, you must stop drinking alcohol,"[31] say doctors at the Mayo Clinic. Many patients require drug or behavior therapy at a clinic to help them stop drinking. Some participate in groups like Alcoholics Anonymous.

In some cases, doctors also prescribe short-term treatment with corticosteroids to reduce liver inflammation. Pentoxifylline, a medication that improves blood flow and decreases the production of cytokines that worsen inflammation, can also be used in people who have severe liver damage.

## Treatment of Nonalcoholic Steatohepatitis

There is no specific treatment for NASH, though obese people with fatty liver who gradually lose weight and take medications like metformin or pioglitazone to decrease insulin resistance can often decrease fat in the liver and thus improve any NASH symptoms, as well as halt the progression of scarring and cirrhosis. Doctors say it is important for any weight loss to occur

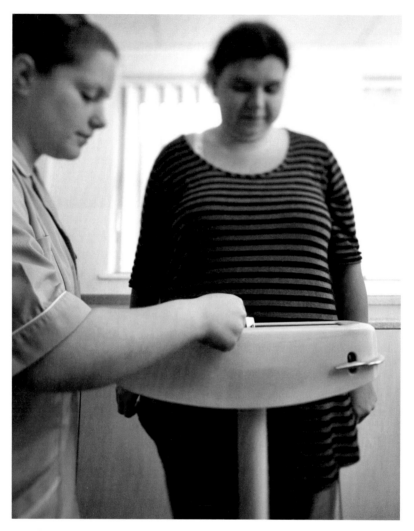

Gradual weight loss, combined with medication to decrease insulin resistance, can decrease fat in the liver, improving NASH symptoms.

gradually, since sudden weight loss can increase liver inflammation. This is because the liver is responsible for breaking down lost fat. When sudden and extreme weight loss occurs, the liver may not be able to process all the lost fat, and this fat may accumulate in the liver and further inflame it.

In addition to weight loss, doctors say that avoiding alcohol can help alleviate symptoms and liver damage in NASH.

## Treatment for Toxic Hepatitis

There is also no specific treatment for toxic hepatitis, except in the case of acetaminophen overdose. In those instances, a drug called N-acethycysteine can minimize liver damage if given within eight hours of the overdose. The only treatment for other toxin-induced hepatitis is putting someone in the hospital to receive intravenous fluids until they recover, discontinuing the offending medication, and stopping exposure to a poison. Sometimes the liver heals, but this can take many months. In other cases, the damage is irreversible and can lead to liver failure.

## Treatment for Hepatitis Complications

In addition to treatments that aim to cure or control the various forms of hepatitis, some patients require therapy for complications of the disease. The primary complication, cirrhosis, cannot be treated, but successfully treating the hepatitis can often slow or halt further liver scarring. Other complications, such as bleeding in the esophagus, can sometimes be treated with drugs called beta blockers. These medications lower blood pressure and thus reduce the amount of blood flowing into the veins. But often patients need blood transfusions, injections of chemicals that burn the bleeding area to stop bleeding, or surgical procedures where doctors tie a rubber band around bleeding blood vessels or insert a hollow tube through the jugular vein into the liver to drain backed-up blood.

Ascites can sometimes be treated with a low-salt diet that diminishes fluid retention. If this does not work, the patient can take medications like spironolactone or furosemide to drain fluid. Sometimes doctors must insert a needle into the abdomen or implant a tube to keep fluid draining.

Patients with hepatic encephalopathy often benefit from a low protein diet, since proteins can cause bacteria in the intestines to produce high levels of ammonia and other toxins that a diseased liver cannot process. Drugs like lactulose and neomycin can also help. Lactulose increases the amount of acid in the intestines, and this kills ammonia-producing bacteria. Neomycin directly kills these same bacteria.

## An Important Part of Any Treatment

An important part of any treatment for hepatitis or its complications is good nutrition and exercise. A healthy diet provides essential nutrients that help the liver heal, and regular exercise helps a patient maintain his or her strength during treatment and recovery. Some patients are not well enough to exercise, but doctors say that those who can should try to do daily aerobic and strength-enhancing exercises. Even taking a daily walk can help.

A healthy diet includes adequate amounts of protein, fat, complex carbohydrates (like grains, rice, or pasta), and limited amounts of processed foods that contain excessive sugar, fat, and salt. However, experts caution that anyone with hepatitis should limit the amount of protein to 20–30 percent of the daily diet, since a damaged liver cannot process too much protein. Most of this protein should be from vegetable rather than meat sources, since meats contain more potentially toxic chemicals. For this reason, people with hepatitis should not consume protein shakes or supplements either.

Liver specialists say most people with hepatitis should not take vitamin or mineral supplements because of the potential for overburdening the liver. Sometimes doctors prescribe such supplements for people who do not eat well, and some studies indicate that vitamin C and E supplements actually lessen liver inflammation. However, experts caution against using these supplements without medical supervision.

## Alternative Treatments

Because standard hepatitis treatments are costly, often ineffective, and have unpleasant side effects, many patients seek alternative therapies such as special diets or herbal supplements. These treatments are not accepted by the traditional medical community. Although some of them are safe and appear to

Milk thistle extract has been used since ancient times for liver ailments. Present-day herbalists recommend it to help the liver process toxins and reduce inflammation.

help some people, many are without merit and are even dangerous. "'Natural' or diet treatments and herbal remedies can be quite dangerous, and no herbal, diet, supplement, or alternative medicine has been scientifically proven to curee—or even ease—symptoms of hepatitis,"[32] says Hepatitis Foundation International.

Doctors say patients should be especially wary of so-called miracle cures touted in books, on the Internet, and in other media, even if the individual recommending the "cure" claims to be a doctor. One such treatment that has been widely promoted is the "liver cleansing" diet. Hepatologist Howard Worman warns: "'Liver cleansing' has no medical or scientific meaning. There is no general 'liver diet' or any diet to keep the liver 'clean' or 'healthy'."[33]

There is one widely touted herb that does, however, seem safe and effective. People have used milk thistle since ancient times to treat liver ailments. It is presently approved for the treatment of hepatitis in some countries, but not in the United States. Some Americans take it anyway, and herbalists who recommend it say the active ingredient, silymarin, helps the liver process toxins and reduces liver inflammation. Some studies have shown it also relieves nausea and fatigue. Further studies are underway to determine whether milk thistle is truly beneficial.

## When the Liver Fails

When hepatitis is not treated or if treatment fails, end-stage liver disease and liver failure can result. A patient may then need a liver transplant to survive. Some patients are not eligible for a liver transplant. For example, people with liver cancer that has spread or those who continue to drink alcohol cannot receive a new liver.

Doctors have performed thousands of liver transplants since 1967, when Thomas Starzl of the University of Colorado did the first successful procedure. However, many more people need transplants than there are available liver donors, so physicians

The most commonly used transplant technique is orthotopic transplantation, in which the native liver is removed and replaced by the donor organ in the same anatomical location as the original liver.

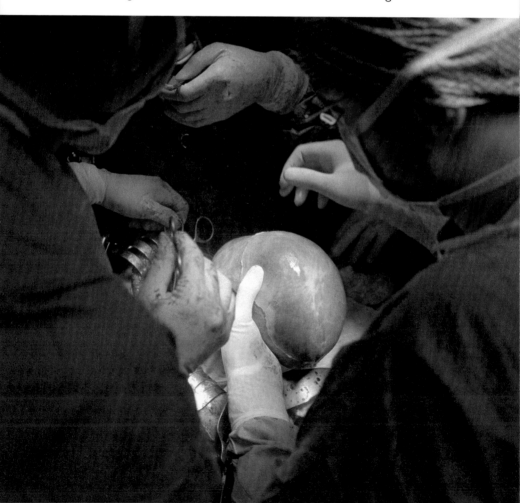

put patients' names on a waiting list. "When a doctor estimates that the patient cannot live more than two years without a new liver, he or she will enter the patient's name on the waiting list,"[34] explain the authors of *The Cleveland Clinic Guide to Liver Disorders*. There are presently more than 15,000 people in the United States on waiting lists, and many will die before a compatible donor who shares the same blood type and other body chemistry is found, even though the National Organ Procurement Organization (OPO) ranks patients on these lists according to how sick they are.

There has been controversy about the ranking of patients because some critics claim that wealthy people able to pay the necessary $100,000 to $200,000 for a transplant have received priority, even though others were sicker and laws prohibit this practice. Another controversy exists about the wisdom of performing liver transplants in people with alcoholic hepatitis who have stopped drinking. The Mayo Clinic explains the controversy:

> Some medical centers may be reluctant to perform liver transplants on people with alcoholic liver disease because they believe a substantial number will return to drinking after surgery, won't take the necessary anti-rejection medicationsdrugs that suppress the immune system so it will not destroy donated tissue, or will require more care and resources than will other patients. Most of these objections have not been borne out in practice, however, and many doctors now feel that some people with alcoholic liver disease are good candidates for transplant surgery. But requirements are still stringent, including abstinence from alcohol for at least six months before surgery and enrollment in a counseling program.[35]

Notwithstanding the controversies, when a suitable donor is found, a hospitalized patient whose name is first on the transplant list will be rushed into surgery. Patients who are not in the hospital must always carry a pager or cell phone so they

# Controversies About Wealth and Liver Transplants

A great deal of controversy about the selection of patients for liver transplants existed before 2002. Many people claimed that fame or financial status, rather than medical need, often determined who received the first available liver. In 1995, for example, baseball star Mickey Mantle 's liver was failing from hepatitis C, forty years of alcohol abuse, and liver cancer. Mantle had stopped drinking alcohol, but liver cancer would have prevented most patients from being approved for a transplant. However, doctors at Baylor Medical Center in Dallas found Mantle a suitable liver in two days and performed the transplant. Mantle died three months later from the cancer, and many critics claimed he only received the transplant because of his wealth and fame.

In 2002 the United States Department of Health and Human Services instituted the Model for End-Stage Liver Disease (MELD) score as the basis for prioritizing the liver transplant lists maintained by the national Organ Procurement and Transplantation Network. The MELD score reveals how likely it is that a patient will die within three months without a transplant and insures that the sickest

can be notified by local OPO coordinators that they need to immediately get to a transplant center.

Surgeons can perform two types of transplants. Both are complicated operations that can last from four to twelve hours. A complete liver transplant places a whole, healthy liver from a newly deceased or brain-dead donor inside the recipient after doctors remove the recipient's diseased liver. A living donor transplant takes a large piece of a live donor's liver and implants it into the recipient. Both liver pieces then regenerate into complete livers within a few weeks.

patients get the first transplants, regardless of how long they have been on a list or whether or not they have financial resources.

However, critics argue that some wealthy people still receive priority because they have the money to travel to multiple transplant centers throughout the country and secure placement on multiple lists. When Apple Computer CEO Steve Jobs received a liver transplant in 2009 in Memphis, Tennessee, even though he lived in California, many medical ethicists claimed that Jobs's wealth enabled him to travel to a transplant center with a shorter waiting list than those in California. However, such practices are not illegal, and transplant administrators say there is little that can be done to stop them.

Apple founder Steve Jobs received a liver transplant in Tennessee, even though he lived in California.

Many patients' new livers function well and allow them to live for many years. About 55 percent of liver transplant patients are alive ten years after the procedure. But sometimes the recipient's body rejects a donated liver despite the antirejection drugs that all transplant patients must take, and this can lead to death.

While liver transplants and other modern treatment options have improved survival for many people with hepatitis, uncertainty over whether treatment will be successful and difficulties with side effects can make living with the disease and its therapy challenging, despite these technological advances.

# CHAPTER FIVE

# Living with Hepatitis

Living with hepatitis and its treatment can be both physically and emotionally challenging. People with chronic hepatitis are most likely to be forced to make a variety of changes in their lives, but those with severe acute hepatitis may face similar challenges.

## Reactions to Diagnosis

Emotional distress can begin before diagnosis if troubling symptoms lead an individual to suspect something is wrong. Then, when a doctor diagnoses hepatitis, fear and uncertainty may be heightened because of the unpredictable nature of the disease and tension about infecting others with contagious forms.

Most people are shocked by a diagnosis of hepatitis. Many initially deny that they are sick, but most eventually come to accept their condition. Michelle, who was diagnosed with HBV, went through a typical emotional roller coaster. "After my diagnosis I experienced the emotional succession of denial, depression, and then acceptance,"[36] she said.

It took Rudolpho, though, quite awhile to accept his condition. "I avoided getting a liver biopsy for almost a year because I was in denial. I didn't want to face the fact that my life would be permanently changed by this."[37]

Some patients are relieved by a diagnosis because they finally know what they are up against. Alan, who experienced fatigue and body aches for two years before doctors diagnosed him with HCV, said, "Of course, I was devastated by the news, but in some ways it was a relief to finally find out what was causing the severe fatigue."[38]

For others, the uncertainty and fear over the future can be overwhelming, as Carol found out when her doctor told her she had HCV. "What goes through one's mind when they are told they have a potentially life-threatening disease? Well, my mind had me dying at any moment and I was overwhelmed with feelings that my life had been cut very short."[39]

## Ways of Coping

Patients and health care experts say there are several things people can do to help them deal with the fear and uncertainty that follow diagnosis and often persist well beyond. All these strategies involve taking charge of things in life that can be controlled. This diminishes feelings of powerlessness and may even increase the chances of getting better. For example, patients can start living healthier lives by eating a healthier diet, exercising if possible, and stopping high-risk behaviors like drinking alcohol, taking illegal drugs, and having unsafe sex. Obtaining accurate information about hepatitis can also help. Researching the disease in legitimate books and websites and asking questions at doctor visits can often banish unfounded fears or lead a patient to be realistic about the future.

Support groups play an important role for patients by helping them gain increased confidence and acceptance of their liver disease through the knowledge that they share a common struggle.

Choosing a caring and competent doctor is another thing that can help make living with hepatitis easier. Some patients' insurance plans do not allow them to choose their doctor, but many people have the option of finding a physician who is concerned and is knowledgeable about the disease. Local hospitals, medical societies, and national advocacy groups like the American Liver Foundation can recommend good liver specialists.

Patients can also get recommendations from local hepatitis support groups, and these and online support groups can help with coping with the disease as well. Support groups consist of people with certain diseases or problems getting together to share knowledge and compassion. Some groups sponsor lectures by health care experts or participate in advocacy and fundraising. Many people benefit immensely from support groups. "The proven healing power of support groups comes from peo-

# The Benefits of Support Groups

Many people find that support groups help them cope with the challenges of living with hepatitis. Jake, for example, wrote, "I went to a weekly support group and this helped immensely to hear and speak with others in the same condition. It gave me hope to hear their stories and how they coped with their illness. I also got the opportunity to take care of others emotionally – at times just by listening and sometimes through sharing my own experiences. Through my group I found out about acupuncture and massage which were invaluable in helping me deal with the treatment side effects, especially the headaches. I also began to meditate each morning – this helped to accept my circumstances and face each day with some level of hope and joy."

Quoted in Hepatitis C Support Project. "Jake." www.hcvadvocate.org/community/stories/Jake.pdf.

ple with similar problems sharing their strength, hopes, and experiences,"[40] explains Hepatitis Foundation International. Talking with supportive family members and friends can also help with coping.

## All About Attitude

Many people find that changing their attitude and helping others contribute greatly to making life with hepatitis easier and more meaningful. A young woman in Guatemala found that developing a positive attitude helped her cope and, in addition, motivated her to work toward a career in hepatitis research that she hoped would improve hepatitis care in her country. She wrote:

> "I spent many years crying, complaining, blaming and playing the role of victim, until I realized that there are just two solutions for situations like this: you sit and cry or you enjoy the beauty of being alive and make every day count. I decided on the second choice. The day I can help to make sure that my country can provide free hepatitis B screenings, vaccines, and affordable treatments, I will feel that I did not pass through a couple of inconveniences in my life for nothing,"[41]

Several celebrities who have hepatitis found that using their fame to promote hepatitis awareness and research helped them cope personally as well. Country singer Naomi Judd, who retired from her singing career in 1991 because of HCV, became an American Liver Foundation spokesperson and works tirelessly to educate the public. "Even though I was quite ill, I wanted to see something positive come from such a crisis. The word crisis in Chinese is made up of 2 characters: danger and opportunity,"[42] she wrote on her website.

Teenaged celebrity Jazzy de Lisser founded a charity called Liver Good Life to raise funds for hepatitis research and released a video diary about her struggles to let the public know about the toll HCV takes on its victims. She also spoke out about how

Since birth, seventeen-year-old Jazzy de Lisser has suffered from hepatitis C. In order to change people's perceptions and raise awareness of the disease, she has made a film about her life and her treatment.

the stigma of having hepatitis affected her deeply. "It's a disease that's very hard to relate to and it's embarrassing. If someone told me about having Hepatitis C and I didn't know much about it, I would be freaked out as well. I'm always scared of how people, boys, will react,"[43] she told CNN.

## Stigma and Discrimination

Because some types of hepatitis are transmitted sexually or through illegal drug use, the disease in general carries a stigma that can lead to paranoid reactions from others or even to discrimination. Joanna, a nurse, described how her coworkers reacted when she told them she had HBV. "The atmosphere in the room changed instantly. The nurses visibly shrank from me as though I were a leper and my head nurse, looking grave, said

# Tips for Developing a Positive Attitude

Registered nurse Lucinda K. Porter offers some tips for helping patients develop a positive attitude that can make living with hepatitis easier:

- Be honest and realistic. Do not base your attitude on thinking things are worse than they are or better than they are.

- Make sure you know the truth. Get accurate information.

- Stay in the present. Don't make things worse by imagining a future with pain, disability or loss.

- Accept your situation.

- Maintain your perspective. Focus your attention on something that brings peace, joy, laughter and meaning.

- Watch your words. If you hear yourself talking negatively, substitute positive phrases.

- Try to relax. Tell yourself that difficult moments will pass.

- Visualize health, not illness.

- Practice gratitude. Make it a habit to find things for which you are grateful.

- Learn what you can control and what you cannot.

- Help others. When it comes to stepping outside of ourselves, probably nothing works as well as reaching out to others who are also struggling.

Lucinda K. Porter. "Stigma and Hepatitis C." www.hcvadvocate.org/hepatitis/factsheets_pdf/stigma_09.pdf.

that I'd probably be off work for a long time. It was surprising how little we knew about the disease."[44]

Sometimes even telling family members about hepatitis can lead to unfortunate consequences because of stigma and misinformation about how the disease is spread. "A patient of mine who was diagnosed with hepatitis C and shared this information with her family was devastated when her daughter prohibited her from hugging or cuddling her granddaughter. Another patient was literally told to leave his home by his wife,"[45] wrote Sanjiv Chopra in *Dr. Sanjiv Chopra's Liver Book*.

Stigma and misinformation can lead to discrimination in some cases. The federal Americans With Disabilities Act of 1992 prohibits employers and other people from discriminating against or firing people with certain disabilities or illnesses as long as the individual is not a danger to others. However, discrimination and job termination often occur anyway. Donna, for example, was fired from her job as a billing supervisor in a medical office because her coworkers feared she would infect them with HCV. This was illegal because Donna's job did not place her at risk of infecting anyone. Some people sue their employers for such actions, but many lack the knowledge or financial resources to do so. One such legal case resulted in a restaurant having to pay a cook $50,000 after the cook sued because he was fired for having HCV. The court ruled that he should not have been fired because HCV is not spread through food.

Other forms of discrimination occur in situations like health care settings. Some doctors and dentists refuse to treat people with viral hepatitis, even though this is prohibited under the Americans With Disabilities Act unless the practitioner can prove that the person poses a risk. One man with HCV reported that three dentists would not treat him before he finally found one who would. A woman named Jeanie had a similar experience when she went to a laboratory for blood tests. "The tech that was supposed to do my blood did not want to do it and then the one who attempted poked me 5 times because she was afraid to touch me,"[46] she explained.

Because of such experiences, many people with hepatitis avoid telling others that they are sick. However, some state laws require individuals with contagious diseases to disclose their condition to others such as health care workers who are at risk of exposure. Experts also emphasize that it is important for people to inform family members and friends so they can take precautions to avoid becoming infected.

## Dealing with the Physical Challenges

The physical as well as emotional challenges can make living with hepatitis difficult. Fatigue, pain, nausea, and other symptoms can force people to cut back on activities or even stop working or going to school. Valene, who began HCV treatment at age fourteen, was distressed when interferon and ribavirin made her so ill that she could not attend school and had to have home tutoring. The worst part, she said, was feeling isolated from her friends. David, who had to stop working as he underwent treatment, felt useless and suffered financial problems because the government disability payments he received were not enough to cover his expenses, especially with the high cost of treatment drugs.

Acupuncture is a traditional Chinese practice that uses needles to restore an energy flow through specific points on the skin. It is said to relieve pain and is used to treat a wide range of disorders.

Many patients find that limiting tiring activities and resting frequently allows them to continue to lead reasonably fulfilling lives. Joanna, for example, said, "Over time, through repeated bad experiences, I learned to store up energy by staying in bed a certain length of time before doing anything, and then to rest up afterwards."[47] Other people find that arranging flexible hours at work, job sharing, or telecommuting allows them to continue working when they need extra rest.

Methods of making life more tolerable when nausea and loss of appetite are a problem include eating frequent small meals instead of three large ones. For debilitating pain, many people find that relaxation techniques like meditation and massage do wonders. Acupuncture also helps many patients. This is an ancient Chinese medical practice in which doctors insert fine needles into various spots on the skin to balance the body's energy. It is proven to be effective for treating pain and is becoming increasingly popular in Western countries.

When hepatitis treatment is successful, of course, this improves a person's life in general as well as taking away physical suffering. "I've found that "responders" to treatment also appear to have a significant improvement in their quality of life, not only because their symptoms have improved but because worries about their health, fears about infecting others, work-related concerns, and uncertainty about the future also abate,"[48] says Sanjiv Chopra.

## Children and Hepatitis

The physical and emotional challenges from hepatitis are difficult for everyone, but children with the disease face unique problems. Those who are too young to understand their condition may be puzzled and overly upset about painful tests and treatments. Helen, whose daughter Morgan was diagnosed with HBV after Helen and her husband adopted Morgan from China, described Morgan's first liver biopsy at age fourteen months.

One of the most difficult things to do was sit with Morgan for nine hours while depriving her of food before the procedure. She went from being a happy baby, to a quiet, withdrawn baby wondering why we wouldn't feed her. I'll never forget carrying my little one into the operating room and trying to soothe her as they placed the mask over her face. Later, we could hear her screaming as we entered the recovery room.[49]

Interferon injections and frequent blood tests were traumatic for Morgan and her parents as well.

Tests and treatment can be difficult for older children too. Valene, who started taking interferon at age fourteen, said, "It was so upsetting to find out that my parents and me would have to give me my shots at home."[50]

Many children also suffer socially because other kids tease or bully them because of their illness. Twelve year-old Billy described what happened to him: "Last year when I was on shots and missed a lot of school, some kids teased me and called me names. One time I couldn't play a sport because the coach thought I might hurt other kids. That hurt me really bad."[51]

Experts say it is important for parents to encourage children with hepatitis to talk about any physical or emotional trauma and to try to lead as normal a life as possible when their condition allows.

## Family Challenges

Those who support family members who have hepatitis also face challenges. Kyle, a teenager in Chico, California, was overwhelmed when he had to take care of his mother for six months while she was incapacitated from HCV treatment. In addition to going to school, Kyle had to clean, cook, and take care of the family's dogs and cats. "It made me mature really fast. I think it'll help me out in the long run,"[52] he said in a newspaper interview. He coped by riding his bicycle to relax and, in fact, improved his mountain biking skills so much that he went on to win numerous races.

Other family members face emotional, lifestyle, and financial disruptions as well when they must assist a sick loved one

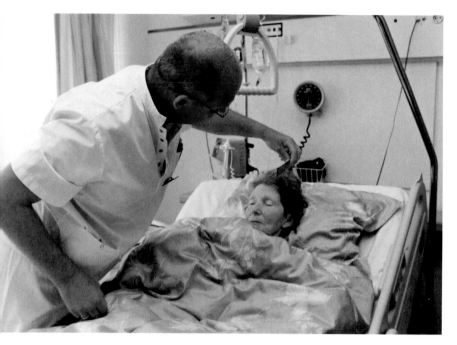

Hospice care is the active total care of a patient with a terminal disease such as terminal hepatitis. Along with the patient's physical health, it involves caring for the mental and spiritual well-being of both the patient and the family.

with everyday tasks or when a sick head of household cannot work. Life can be especially stressful if the person with hepatitis has alcohol or drug abuse problems. Organizations like Al Anon and Alateen sponsor support programs for adults and teens with alcoholic family members, and these programs help many people cope.

The most difficult time for family members and patients is often when hepatitis treatment fails and nothing more can be done. Patients and their families must make difficult decisions about end of life care, including what lifesaving procedures should be performed if the patient loses consciousness. The patient's wishes can be formalized in legal documents called advance directives or living wills.

Some people choose to spend their final days in a hospital, while others choose to remain at home or stay in a hospice.

A hospice is a facility that specializes in providing comfort, guidance, and care for terminally ill people and their families. Sometimes hospice workers such as nurses, doctors, and counselors come to a patient's home to care for him or her.

When a person with hepatitis dies, family members' grief may be compounded by anger at the patient for contracting hepatitis from alcohol, illegal drugs, or unsafe sex. Sometimes anger at doctors or insurance companies for making mistakes or failing to pay for treatment makes losing a loved one more difficult. Judy, for example, resented the fact that doctors failed to diagnose the HCV of her fiancé, James, for several years after he started having continuous flu-like symptoms. By the time he was diagnosed, James had jaundice and internal bleeding and needed a liver transplant. But he had no medical insurance, and his doctors told him he would have to pay $150,000 to get a transplant. He did not have the money and died a few weeks later. "I believe that if the doctors had done blood work years ago and found out he had hep C, been responsible and cared, he wouldn't have needed $150,000 cash, and would still be alive today,"[53] Judy said.

Because of unhappy endings like this, and because hepatitis makes life so challenging for so many people, advocacy groups and researchers are striving to improve hepatitis care and treatment in hopes of giving patients a brighter future.

# CHAPTER SIX

# The Future

**D**espite improvements in diagnosis, prevention, and treatment, hepatitis continues to affect billions of people worldwide, resulting in widespread suffering and death. Current treatments are expensive, have dangerous side effects, and do not work for many people. Many people are ignorant about hepatitis, and often those who should be tested or treated are not. Thus, experts say there is still much work to be done towards diminishing the spread and burden of the disease in the future.

Researchers and public health agencies are engaged in projects to improve education, diagnosis, treatment, and access to care. Most of these projects focus on hepatitis B and C because these types cause the most deaths, but all forms of hepatitis are being addressed.

## Efforts to Improve Education, Prevention, and Access to Treatment

The CDC is involved in numerous projects to improve education, prevention, and access to treatment. They are currently developing nationwide programs that require doctors and local health departments to diligently report cases of hepatitis to federal authorities. They believe this will help prevention and treatment because they can then direct education efforts towards specific people. CDC is also working with state and local health departments to develop education programs for health care and social service providers who work with at-risk people, and they are encouraging officials to mandate HAV and HBV vaccinations for infants and children to promote prevention in places where these vaccinations are not currently required. In addition, CDC is trying to improve access to hepatitis screening tests for at-risk people who are covered by government insurance programs by encouraging increased coverage for such tests.

The United States Department of Veterans Affairs is also involved in education and treatment efforts because of the many military veterans who have hepatitis. One project they have launched seeks to help veterans with HCV become eligible for antiviral treatment for which they are currently ineligible. As the department explains, "About 70% of veterans with CHC-chronic hepatitis C are considered ineligible for antiviral treatment. Most of these patients are excluded due to the presence of co-existing depression and substance abuse."[54] The project offers counseling, antidepression medication, and substance abuse treatment programs. Another project is testing the effectiveness of a program called motivational enhancement therapy in reducing alcohol consumption among veterans with HCV. The program consists of four sessions with a therapist who is trained to help clients recognize that they are responsible for changing their own behavior.

Universities and private organizations are engaged in improving education as well. Researchers at the University of California, Los Angeles, for example, are working with the Friends Community Center to assess how well an educational program works in convincing homeless gay and bisexual men to receive hepatitis vaccines and to practice safe sex. Specially trained nurses are conducting education sessions and administering vaccines, and the researchers will question participants about behavior changes to assess the program's success.

Other education efforts are focusing on teaching HCV patients about the importance of continuing to take prescribed medicines even if they feel better or dislike the side effects. One study in Spain is questioning patients about whether or not they are following their doctor's orders, and, if not, why not. The researchers are also trying to convince patients who

# Research to Improve Diagnosis

Because the liver biopsies needed to assess liver damage are painful, expensive, and invasive, researchers are attempting to find other methods of accurately measuring liver scarring and stiffness. Scientists at Beth Israel Deaconess Medical Center in Boston are testing a new machine called FibroScan® for this purpose. FibroScan® painlessly and noninvasively measures liver stiffness by using a modified form of ultrasound called ultrasound elastography. The device sends a mechanical vibration wave through the liver via a handheld probe. Then, sound waves measure the speed at which the vibration travels, and the machine calculates the stiffness of the liver based on the speed of travel. Doctors have found that the more scarring there is in the liver, the stiffer it is. The researchers are comparing FibroScan® results to those obtained with liver biopsies to check the accuracy of the new method.

Other research at Johann Wolfgang Goethe University Hospitals in Germany is comparing FibroScan® and liver biopsy testing to another new technology called Acoustic Radiation Force Impulse Imaging (ARFI). ARFI also uses ultrasound waves, but these waves are shorter and of higher intensity than those in FibroScan®. The higher intensity allows the sound waves to slightly move sections of the liver. Computers track these movements and convert the results into readings of tissue stiffness.

This diagnostic device allows one to determine the stage of liver fibrosis due to hepatitis C or cirrhosis. The transducer emits ultrasounds, allowing the measurement of the elasticity of the tissues. This technique is safe, painless, and can replace the liver biopsy in certain cases..

stop treatment to resume it to increase the likelihood that they are cured.

## Efforts to Understand Hepatitis Biology

Hand-in-hand with education efforts, many researchers are attempting to improve treatment by better understanding the biology of hepatitis and its complications. Researchers at Rockefeller University in New York are measuring antibodies, cells that produce antibodies, and chemokines in the blood of people with HCV to gain an understanding of how the immune system responds to the virus. They believe that chemokines, which are small cytokines that direct infection-fighting white blood cells to their targets, are critical in this process. "Our hypothesis is that changes in chemokine levels affect the development of an effective immune response against HCV,"[55] the researchers explain. Understanding this process could lead to new methods of treatment that target these chemokines.

Other work on cytokines is focused on hepatitis E. Since HEV is especially dangerous for pregnant women, resulting in a 20–45 percent death rate, scientists in India are studying how the hormone changes that occur during pregnancy interact with certain gene abnormalities to affect cytokines that ordinarily fight HEV. Previous research has indicated that hormone changes dampen the immune response to HEV and that some gene mutations can exacerbate this problem. By identifying these genes and cytokines, doctors hope to develop methods of helping pregnant women fight the disease.

Scientists in Canada and Denmark are studying how HCV affects the brain. Many patients have problems with thinking skills, but thus far no one has identified why this occurs. The researchers are measuring patients' brain structures with magnetic resonance imaging (MRI) technology to see if HCV causes brain damage and are also testing to see if HCV migrates from the liver to the brain.

Other researchers are studying how hepatitis damages the liver. A study at the University Health Network in Canada is investigating how certain genes and blood proteins affect the

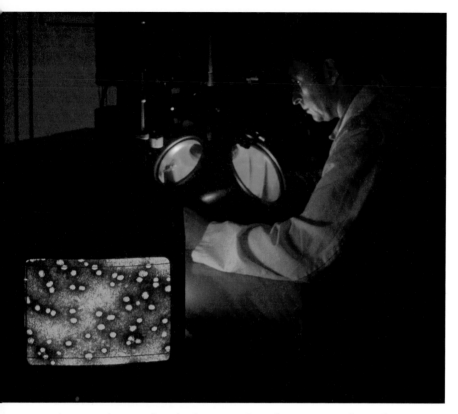

A researcher studies the hepatitis B surface antigen through an electron microscope monitor.

degree of liver damage and patients' response to treatment. Related research at Emory University in Atlanta, Georgia, is try-ing to identify which immune chemicals in the body act to help some people destroy the hepatitis C virus before an acute case becomes chronic. This type of research can help in developing and targeting new treatments for specific classes of patients.

## Research on Response to Treatment

Since doctors do not yet understand why some patients respond well to treatment while others do not, a great deal of research is focused on this topic. Several studies have indi-cated that obesity and insulin resistance play a role, even in viral hepatitis. "Obesity superimposed on CHC reduces the success of antiviral treatment and promotes liver scarring, fatty liver, and increases the risk of liver cancer. IRinsulin resistance, like obesity in CHC, reduces antiviral success rates,"[56] explain researchers at University Health Network in Toronto, Canada. Thus, scientists are testing whether reducing obesity and insulin resistance improves HCV treatment outcome. One study is assessing how well a six-month weight loss and exercise program works in motivating HCV patients to lose weight, and whether any weight loss improves response to treatment. Another study is testing whether reducing insulin resistance with the diabetes drug pioglitazone improves HCV treatment outcomes.

Scientists at the National Taiwan University Hospital, meanwhile, are studying a molecule in the liver and blood called miR-122. This is a micro-RNA molecule, a type of RNA that regulates how another type of RNA called messenger RNA translates genetic information in cells. MiR-122 appears to determine how well the body stops the hepatitis C virus from replicating. Many patients who do not respond well to HCV treatment have low levels of miR-122, and the researchers are trying to find out exactly how it affects the HCV virus in hopes of learning how to manipulate this molecule to improve treatment outcome.

Scientists at the National Institute of Allergy and Infectious Diseases are also studying the role of genes and the immune system in HCV treatment outcome. Previous studies suggest that African Americans tend to respond less favorably to treatment than Caucasians do, and investigators are analyzing differences in genes and immune cells in these two groups to determine whether these factors influence response to treatment.

Since HCV patients with a high viral load are also less likely to respond well to drug treatment, researchers in Taiwan are testing a new method of reducing viral load mechanically. The technique is called double filtration plasmapheresis. Here, doctors connect a patient to a plasmapheresis machine with intravenous tubes. The patient's blood is pumped through the machine, which separates the blood plasma (liquid portion) and blood cells and sends the plasma through a strainer that separates large and small molecules. The large molecules, which include viruses, are discarded, and the smaller molecules, such as proteins, are returned to the patient's body along with the blood cells. This technique does not get rid of all viruses, but it can reduce viral load, and the researchers hope this reduction will be sufficient to improve treatment outcome.

## New Drugs Being Tested

In addition to seeking to improve treatment outcome with existing drugs, researchers are also testing many new drugs and drug combinations to improve hepatitis care. Drug manufacturer Abbott, for example, is conducting clinical trials on several new antiviral drugs. ABT-450 is an oral protease inhibitor designed to block the protease enzyme that allows HCV to replicate. ABT-333 and ABT-072 are oral polymerase inhibitors that block the polymerase enzyme that does the same thing. Although there are already several protease and polymerase inhibitors on the market, scientists keep searching for new compounds that can withstand viruses becoming resistant to them. HCV develops resistance to drugs quickly, and the Abbott researchers are testing these new antiviral drugs alone and in combination with peginterferon and ribavirin to see if they diminish this resistance. They hope that blocking different enzymes involved in virus reproduction with several drugs will increase the chances of disabling the virus before it can mutate. As explained in the publication *Hepatitis C: New Treatments in the Pipeline:* "Hepatitis C treatment requires a combination of drugs that target different steps in the replication cycle."[57]

Two other new protease inhibitors being tested in combination with peginterferon and ribavirin seem to hold great promise for improving HCV treatment as well. Telaprevir, developed by Vertex Pharmaceuticals, and boceprevir, developed by Merck & Company, both cured about 90 percent of the patients who received them in clinical trials, according to reports issued in November 2010. Telaprevir also cut the necessary treatment duration from forty-eight to twenty-four weeks, and boceprevir reduced it from nine months to six months. The

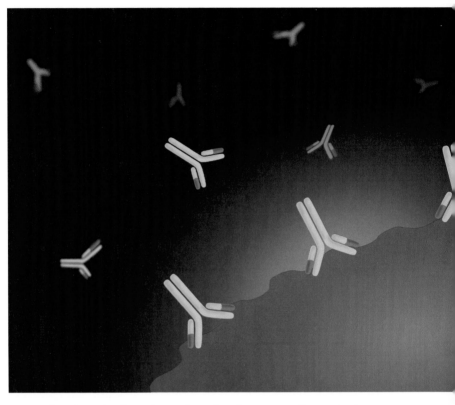

Monoclonal antibodies, shown here binding to a cell, are single antibodies that scientists clone and use to attack specific antigens. Combined with peginterferon and ribavirin, it may improve hepatitis treatment.

manufacturers expect both drugs to be approved by the FDA in the near future, and hepatitis experts have hailed these drugs as important milestones. "You're looking at a major advance in the field of hepatitis,"[58] said Fred Poordad, chief of hepatology at Cedars-Sinai Medical Center in Los Angeles, in a *Boston Globe* interview.

Another drug company, Cytheris SA in France, is currently conducting phase one clinical trials on a new injectible drug called CYT107, or interleukin-7. This is a synthetic cytokine that increases the number of T cells, which are a type of white blood cells that fight infections in the body. Scientists are hoping that adding this drug to existing HBV treatments will improve treatment success for more patients.

In a phase two trial, Novelos Therapeutics is testing another new injectible drug called NOV-205 to see if it helps HCV patients who do not respond to standard therapy. Glutathione and inosine, the active ingredients in NOV-205, reduce inflammation and boost the immune system. Glutathione is a naturally occurring antioxidant found in body cells. It helps protect cells from damaging substances called free radicals, detoxifies some toxins, and enhances the immune system. Inosine is found in cells' RNA and is important in translating the genetic code and helping to kill viruses. Thus far, results with NOV-205 appear promising.

Another type of injectible drug being tested is monoclonal antibodies. These are single antibodies that scientists clone and use to attack specific antigens. Researchers at the Cleveland Clinic are testing a monoclonal antibody called infliximab to see if it improves HCV treatment outcome when combined with peginterferon and ribavirin. Infliximab is currently used to treat some autoimmune diseases because it decreases inflammation. But it also depresses the immune system and can thus lead to cancer or infections, so doctors must be very careful about using it. Despite the risks, researchers believe it may do more good than harm in some cases.

Other researchers are exploring new types of interferon treatments. Han All BioPharma of Korea is conducting phase one trials on a new form of interferon called Hanferon to see if it is superior to peginterferon in treating HCV. Hanferon is made by genetically engineering proteins in interferon alpha to make them longer lasting and more resistant to breakdown in the body.

Researchers at Huntington Medical Research Institutes in California are studying whether gamma interferon is effective for treating HBV. Like other interferons, gamma interferon stimulates the immune system, but it works by binding to different cell receptors than other interferons do. It seems to have stronger effects on the immune system's ability to recognize and attack viruses and also seems to have less intense side effects than interferon alpha does, so scientists are hoping it may offer a more effective and less unpleasant method of treating hepatitis B.

In research on new drugs for nonviral forms of hepatitis, scientists are testing whether the steroids budesonide and deflazacort can reduce inflammation in AIH. These steroids do not have as many side effects as the prednisone currently used to treat the disease, and preliminary trials show that both drugs may be effective in treating AIH.

## Combinations and New Uses for Drugs

Many studies are evaluating whether new combinations of existing drugs or drugs currently used for other purposes can improve hepatitis treatment. For example, NIDDK is testing whether combining the antiviral drugs tenofovir and emtricitabine is more effective than using these drugs alone to treat HBV.

Several research teams are investigating whether statin drugs like simvastatin, currently used to lower cholesterol, can reduce viral load in people with HBV and HCV alone or in combination with standard antiviral drugs. Previous studies showed that statins inhibit HBV and HCV virus replication in test tubes, and scientists are hoping that these widely used drugs will help hepatitis patients as well.

Other researchers are testing the effectiveness of the high blood pressure medications candesartan and irbesartan in reducing liver scarring in people with many types of hepatitis. These drugs work by blocking the hormone angiotensin, which tightens blood vessels. Blocking the hormone thus reduces blood pressure. Angiotensin also appears to activate stellate cells in the liver that produce scar tissue, so the investigators hypothesize that blocking this hormone may be a method of safely and effectively reducing scar tissue formation.

Since insulin resistance and type 2 diabetes often contribute to NASH, several researchers funded by NIDDK's NASH Clinical Research Network are evaluating whether insulin resistance–reducing medications like metformin and rosiglita-zone can decrease liver inflammation in NASH patients. Other researchers are studying whether antioxidants like vitamin E and selenium can help reduce inflammation as well.

A number of scientists are studying whether other vitamin, mineral, or herbal supplements can safely enhance treatment for all types of hepatitis. A study at the University of Maryland, for example, is testing whether silymarin, the active ingredient in the widely touted herb milk thistle, affects liver enzymes and speeds healing in people with HAV. Researchers in Israel are evaluating whether vitamin D supplements can strengthen the immune system and safely improve treatment success in HCV patients. Another Israeli team is testing whether omega-3 fatty acids, which many people take to reduce depression and high cholesterol, can help prevent the depression that many hepatitis patients experience as a side effect of interferon treatment.

## New Types of Treatment

In addition to evaluating new drug treatments, researchers are exploring entirely new methods of treating hepatitis. Some doctors are developing new liver and liver cell transplant procedures. One new method is split-liver transplantation. Here, surgeons divide a deceased or brain-dead donor's liver into two parts. Each part is transplanted into a different recipient and regenerates into a whole liver. Not only does this allow transplants for two patients, but it also allows doctors to cut the liver into sizes that fit specific patients like children, who need smaller livers or liver pieces than adults do. Thus far, the procedure seems to work as well as standard liver transplants do.

Another experimental procedure is called an auxiliary transplant. Here, surgeons transplant a small piece of a live donor's liver into a patient whose liver is failing, without removing the patient's diseased liver. Doctors have been attempting this procedure since the 1980s but rarely have had positive results, so they are trying to improve the technique so it can help more people.

In another new procedure called hepatocyte transplantation, doctors inject a healthy donor's liver cells into a patient with liver failure. This appears to improve liver function in laboratory animals, and early tests with humans are under way. A similar technique called stem cell transplantation is being

Scientists are developing methods of programming stem cells to develop into certain cells like hepatocytes, then infusing millions of these cells into hepatitis patients in hopes that the cells will migrate to and repair the liver.

# Testing New Drugs

Researchers initially develop new drugs in a laboratory and test safety and effectiveness on laboratory animals. Once a drug passes these tests, doctors begin testing, called clinical trials, on human volunteers. The Food and Drug Administration (FDA) in the United States and comparable agencies in other countries regulate all aspects of drug testing and approval.

Three phases of clinical trials must be successfully completed before FDA will approve a drug for sale. In phase one, a small group of patients, usually no more than ten or twenty, receive the new drug to determine safe, effective doses. In phase two, a larger group of about one hundred people are given the drug over several years to test safety and effectiveness. Phase three involves thousands of patients being randomly assigned to either an experimental or a control group. Those in the experimental group receive the new drug, while those in the control group receive a placebo, or fake, that looks like the real thing. This way doctors can assess whether any positive results are due to the expectation of success rather than to the drug itself.

If a drug's benefits outweigh its risks and it is approved, sometimes drug manufacturers arrange phase four, or postmarket studies, to learn about long-term effects or to test the drug on another illness.

studied to see if injecting or infusing stem cells through a vein can repair a diseased liver. Stem cells are immature cells that have the ability to develop into many different types of cells in the body. They can be obtained from embryos, umbilical cord blood, live donor blood, or from a patient's own blood and grown in a laboratory. Scientists are developing methods of programming stem cells to develop into certain cells like hepatocytes, and then are infusing millions of these cells into hepatitis patients in hopes that the cells will migrate to and repair the liver. However, much more testing is needed before doctors know whether this is safe and effective.

Another innovation that may help people with hepatitis is a liver-assist device. This is a machine designed to remove toxins from the blood and make essential proteins to keep a patient with a failing liver alive until he or she can receive a liver transplant. The device, known as the Extracorporeal Liver Assist Device, contains special cartridges filled with functioning hepatocytes. A patient is connected to the machine with intravenous tubes, and his or her blood is pumped through the machine and returned after toxins are removed. Thus far, the technique seems to help some patients but not others.

## Hope for the Future

The goal of all this research is to improve prevention, diagnosis, and treatment of all forms of hepatitis so they will no longer cause widespread suffering and death. Although medical science has a long way to go before hepatitis can be universally cured or prevented, the authors of *The Cleveland Clinic Guide to Liver Disorders* express the medical community's optimism for the future: "Science and technology are advancing rapidly, and so are our successes in treating and preventing these diseases."[59]

# Notes

## Introduction: Hepatitis: A Frightening Disease

1. Institute of Medicine. "FAQs About Hepatitis." http://iom.edu/Reports/2010/Hepatitis-and-Liver-Cancer-A-National-Strategy-for-Prevention-and-Control-of-Hepatitis-B-and-C/Hepatitis-Quiz.aspx.
2. Centers for Disease Control. "Hepatitis and Liver Cancer: A National Strategy for Prevention and Control of Hepatitis B and C." www.cdc.gov/hepatitis/IOMnews.htm.
3. Quoted in John Kerry, U.S. Senator for Massachusetts. "Kerry Introduces Bill to Fight Viral Hepatitis." http://Kerry.senate.gov/press/release/?id=77720c93-e5db-46a3-b02f-9bfe1814b4c7.

## Chapter One: What Is Hepatitis?

4. World Health Organization. "Hepatitis A." www.who.int/mediacentre/factsheets/fs328/en/index.html.
5. Nizar N. Zein and Kevin M. Edwards. *The Cleveland Clinic Guide to Liver Disorders*. New York: Kaplan Publishing, 2009, p. 17.
6. Nizar N. Zein and Kevin M. Edwards. *The Cleveland Clinic Guide to Liver Disorders*, p. 4.
7. Hepatitis Foundation International. "Caring for Your Liver," www.hepfi.org/living/liv_caring.html.
8. Quoted in Experience Project. "I Have Autoimmune Hepatitis – Guides: What is it Like to Have Autoimmune Hepatitis." www.experienceproject.com/guides/what-is-it-like-to-have-Autoimmine-Hepatitis/89362.
9. Melissa Palmer. *Dr. Melissa Palmer's Guide to Hepatitis & Liver Disease*, New York: Avery, 2004, p. 16.

## Chapter Two: Causes and Risk Factors

10. Melissa Palmer. *Dr. Melissa Palmer's Guide to Hepatitis & Liver Disease*, p. 75.
11. Centers for Disease Control. "Overview and Statistics." www.cdc.gov/hepatitis/HAV/HAVfaq.htm.
12. Hepatitis Foundation International. "Hepatitis B." www.hepfi.org/pdfs/HBV%201.pdf.
13. Centers for Disease Control. "Correctional Facilities and Viral Hepatitis." www.cdc.gov/hepatitis/Settings/corrections.htm.
14. Centers for Disease Control. "Hepatitis C FAQs for Health Professionals." www.cdc.gov/hepatitis/HCV/HCVfaq.htm#section2.
15. Quoted in Hepatitis C Support Project. "Jake." www.hcvadvocate.org/community/stories/Jake.pdf.
16. Quoted in National Hepatitis C Coalition. "Debbie's Story." http://nationalhepatitis-c.org/stories/15.htm.
17. Hepatitis Foundation International. "Two Cautions." www.hepfi.org/living/liv_two.html.
18. National Institute of Diabetes and Digestive and Kidney Diseases. "Nonalcoholic Steatohepatitis." http://digestive.niddk.nih.gov/ddiseases/pubs/nash/.

## Chapter Three: Prevention

19. Centers for Disease Control. "Overview and Statistics." www.cdc.gov/hepatitis/HAV/HAVfaq.htm#general.
20. National Institute of Diabetes and Digestive and Kidney Diseases. "Viral Hepatitis: A through E and Beyond." http://digestive.niddk.nih.gov/ddiseases/pubs/viralhepatitis/.
21. John Bathelow Classen. "Clustering of Cases of IDDM 2 to 4 Years After Hepatitis B Immunization Is Consistent with Clustering after Infections and Progression to IDDM in Autoantibody Positive Individuals." The Open Pediatric Medicine Journal vol. 2, 2008, pp. 1–6.
22. Centers for Disease Control. "FAQs About Hepatitis B Vaccine (Hep B) and Multiple Sclerosis." www.cdc.gov/vaccinesafety/vaccines/multiplesclerosis_and_hep_b.html.

23. Mayo Clinic. "Alcoholic Hepatitis." www.mayoclinic.com/print/alcoholic-hepatitis/DS00785/MET.

24. Howard J. Worman, *The Liver Disorders and Hepatitis Sourcebook*. New York: McGraw-Hill, 2006, p. 174.

## Chapter Four: Treatment

25. Howard J. Worman. *The Liver Disorders and Hepatitis Sourcebook*, p. 10.

26. Howard J. Worman. *The Liver Disorders and Hepatitis Sourcebook*, p. 10.

27. Howard J. Worman. *The Liver Disorders and Hepatitis Sourcebook*, p. 113.

28. Quoted in Hepatitis C Support Project. "Dee." www.hcvadvocate.org/community/stories/Dee.pdf.

29. Quoted in CNN.com. "Life with Hepatitis C for London's Teenage 'It Girl.'" www.cnn.com/2009/HEALTH/12/24/jazzy.hepatitis.c/index.html.

30. Melissa Palmer. *Dr. Melissa Palmer's Guide to Hepatitis & Liver Disease*, p. 189.

31. Mayo Clinic. "Alcoholic Hepatitis." www.mayoclinic.com/print/alcoholic-hepatitis/DS00785/MET.

32. Hepatitis Foundation International. "Two Cautions." www.hepfi.org/living/liv_two.html.

33. Howard J. Worman. *The Liver Disorders and Hepatitis Sourcebook*, p. 254.

34. Nizar N. Zein and Kevin M. Edward. *The Cleveland Clinic Guide to Liver Disorders*, p. 171.

35. Mayo Clinic. "Alcoholic Hepatitis." www.mayoclinic.com/print/alcoholic-hepatitis/DS00785/MET.

## Chapter Five: Living with Hepatitis

36. Quoted in Hepatitis B Foundation. "Personal Stories: Michelle's Story." www.hepb.org/patients/personal_stories_michelle.htm.

37. Quoted in Hepatitis B Foundation. "Personal Stories: Rudolpho's Story." www.hepb.org/patients/personal_stories_rudolpho.htm.

38. Quoted in Hepatitis C Support Project. "Alan." www.hcvadvocate.org/community/stories/Alan.pdf.

39. Quoted in Hepatitis C Support Project. "Carol." www .hcvadvocate.org/community/stories/carol.pdf.
40. Hepatitis Foundation International. "Find a Support Group." www.hepfi.org/support/support_find.html.
41. Quoted in Hepatitis B Foundation. "Personal Stories – Dreams Can Come True." www.hepb.org/patients/ personal_stories_dreams.htm.
42. Naomi Judd: The Official Website. "Hepatitis C." www. naomijudd.com/hepatitisC.php.
43. Quoted in CNN.com. "Life With Hepatitis C for London's Teenage 'It Girl.'" www.cnn.com/2009/HEALTH/12/24/ jazzy.hepatitis.c/index.html.
44. Quoted in Hepatitis B Foundation. "I Survived Hepatitis B… Twice!" www.hepb.org/pdf/personal_story_Joanna_ James.pdf.
45. Sanjiv Chopra. *Dr. Sanjiv Chopra's Liver Book.* New York: Simon & Schuster, 2001, p. 63.
46. Quoted in National Hepatitis C Coalition. "Jeanie's Story." http://nationalhepatitis-c.org/stories/30.htm.
47. Quoted in Hepatitis B Foundation. "I Survived Hepatitis B… Twice!" www.hepb.org/pdf/personal_story_Joanna_ James.pdf.
48. Sanjiv Chopra. *Dr. Sanjiv Chopra's Liver Book,* p. 91.
49. Quoted in Hepatitis B Foundation. "Personal Stories: Morgan's Story." www.hepb.org/patients/personal_ stories_morgan.htm.
50. Quoted in National Hepatitis C Coalition. "Valene's Story." http://nationalhepatitis-c.org/stories/12.htm.
51. Quoted in Parents of Kids with Infectious Diseases. "Life As a 12-Year-Old with Hepatitis C." www.pkids.org/pdf/ phr/12-07billystory.pdf.
52. Quoted in Thomas Lawrence. "From Challenges to Championship." www.newsreview.com/chico/ content?oid=1462616.
53. Quoted in National Hepatitis C Coalition. "James' Story." http://nationalhepatitis-c.org/stories/11.htm.

## Chapter Six: The Future

54. Clinical Trials.gov. "Hepatitis C Translating Initiatives for Depression into Solutions (HEPTIDES)." http://clinical trials.gov/ct2/show/NCT01143896?recr=Open&cond=%22 Hepatitis%22&rank=51.

55. Clinical Trials.gov. "Hepatitis C Virus and the Humoral Immune System." http://clinicaltrials.gov/ct2/show/NCT0021 9999?recr=Open&cond=%22Hepatitis%22&rank=50.

56. Clinical Trials.gov. "Lifestyle Intervention Targeting Obesity and Insulin Resistance in Chronic Hepatitis C." http:// clinicaltrials.gov/ct2/show/NCT00755742?recr=Open&con d=%22Hepatitis%22&rank=61.

57. Tracy Swan. "Oral Antivirals: HCV Protease and Polymerase Inhibitors." Hepatitis C: New Treatments in the Pipeline. www.thebody.com/content/art46370.html.

58. Quoted in Boston Globe. "Vertex Nearing Goal on Hepatitis C Drug." http://www.boston.com/business/healthcare/ articles/2010/11/02/vertex_nearing_goal_on_hepatitis_c_ drug/

59. Nizar N. Zein and Kevin M. Edwards. *The Cleveland Clinic Guide to Liver Disorders*, p. 205.

# Glossary

**acute:** Short-term or sudden.

**antibodies:** Chemicals produced by the immune system to fight specific antigens.

**antigens:** Foreign substances or organisms that stimulate the immune system to produce antibodies.

**antiviral:** A drug used to treat a virus infection.

**ascites:** Fluid buildup in the abdomen.

**autoimmune:** A condition in which the immune system attacks the body's own cells.

**bilirubin:** A by-product of the breakdown of red blood cells that can build up when the liver is diseased.

**chromosomes:** The wormlike bodies in cells where genes reside.

**chronic:** Long-term.

**cirrhosis:** Advanced scarring of the liver.

**cytokine:** Chemical messenger.

**fibrosis:** Scar tissue.

**fulminant:** Very severe acute hepatitis.

**gene:** Part of a DNA molecule that transmits hereditary information.

**genotype:** The genetic makeup of an organism.

**hepatic encephalopathy:** Inflammation of the brain caused by liver disease.

**hepatitis:** Inflammation of the liver.

**hepatocyte:** Liver cell.

**inflammation:** Irritation or swelling.

**interferon:** A naturally occurring or man-made chemical that combats viruses.

**intravenous:** Delivering medication directly into a vein using a needle.

**jaundice:** Yellowing of the skin and whites of the eyes.

**relapse:** Recurrence of symptoms or infection.

**steatosis:** Fat in the liver.

**vaccine:** Medication used to prevent a disease.

**viral:** Caused by a virus.

**viral load:** A measurement of how severely infected with a virus a patient is.

**virus:** A submicroscopic organism consisting mostly of DNA or RNA.

# Organizations to Contact

**Centers for Disease Control**
1600 Clifton Road
Atlanta, GA 30333
800-232-4636
www.cdc.gov

CDC is a government agency that provides comprehensive information and statistics on all aspects of viral hepatitis for the public and for health care professionals. Also issues timely warnings and advice on hepatitis prevention and treatment on behalf of the U.S. government.

**American Liver Foundation**
75 Marden Lane, Suite 603
New York, NY 10038-4810
800-465-4837 or 212-668-1000
www.liverfoundation.org

The American Liver Foundation is a nonprofit organization that provides easy-to-understand information and advocacy on general liver health and illness, including specific information about hepatitis. Also sponsors and reports on current research.

**Hepatitis Foundation International**
504 Blick Drive
Silver Spring, MD 20904-2901
800-891-0707 or 301-622-4200
www.hepfi.org

Hepatitis Foundation International is the primary nonprofit organization that focuses specifically on informing the public about all aspects of viral hepatitis, including research. Their website has especially informative sections on living with viral hepatitis and on patient advocacy and support.

**National Digestive Diseases Information Clearinghouse**
2 Information Way
Bethesda, MD 20892-3570
800-891-5389
www.digestive.niddk.nih.gov

This National Institutes of Health site coordinates and distributes information from the National Institute of Diabetes and Digestive and Kidney Diseases on a variety of digestive diseases. While most government and nonprofits' sites focus on viral hepatitis, the NIH site provides comprehensive information on all types of hepatitis.

**Hepatitis B Foundation**
3805 Old Easton Road
Doylestown, PA 18902
215-489-4900
www.hepb.org

Hepatitis B Foundation is the only national nonprofit organization devoted solely to providing information, support, research, and advocacy on hepatitis B.

**Hepatitis C Support Project**
P.O. Box 427037
San Francisco, CA 94142
www.hcvadvocate.org

Hepatitis C Support Project's website provides extensive articles, newsletters, and other information to support and educate people with hepatitis C.

# For More Information

## Books

Connie Goldsmith. *Hepatitis (USA Today Health Reports: Diseases and Disorders)*. Connecticut: Twenty-First Century Books, 2010. Written by a nurse for young adults about all aspects of viral hepatitis, including case studies.

Aileen Gallagher. *Hepatitis*. New York: Rosen Publishing, 2005. Part of the Epidemics series written for teens; discusses hepatitis epidemics, treatment, and research.

Jeri Freedman. *Hepatitis B*. New York: Rosen Publishing, 2009. From the Library of Sexual Health series; informs teens about how hepatitis B is spread and how to prevent it.

## Articles

Thomas Lawrence. "From Challenges to Championship." www .newsreview.com/chico/content?oid=1462616.     Inspiring story of a teen who took care of his hepatitis-infected mother.

Katie Charles. "Prevention and Treatment Can Block Worldwide Health Threat Hepatitis with Many Forms." *New York Daily News*, www.nydailynews.com/lifestyle /health/2010/07/21/2010-07-21_prevention_and_ treatment_can_block_worldwide_health_threat_hepatitis_ with_many_f.html. Interview with a prominent doctor discusses the worldwide threat of hepatitis.

*The Telegraph*. "It Girl Jazzy de Lisser, 17, Breaks Taboos on Hepatitis C." www.telegraph.co.uk/health/healthnews/5778426 /It-girl-Jazzy-de-Lisser-17-breaks-taboos-on-hepatitis-C.html. Article about British teen's life with hepatitis C.

Parents of Kids With Infectious Diseases. "Life as a 12 year-old with Hepatitis C." www.pkids.org/pdf/phr/12-07billystory .pdf. Story about living with hepatitis C written by a twelve-year-old boy.

## Websites

**Teens Health from Nemours.** "Hepatitis." http://kidshealth .org/teen/infections/stds/hepatitis.html. Nemours is a nonprofit health education organization that offers doctor-approved articles on health topics for teens. "Hepatitis" discusses all aspects of viral hepatitis.

**Teens Health from Nemours.** "Hepatitis B." http://kidshealth .org/teen/infections/stds/std_hepatitis.html. Information from Nemours on hepatitis B for teens.

**The Medical Institute for Sexual Health**. "Hepatitis B." www.medinstitute.org/public/104.cfm. The Medical Institute for Sexual Health is a nonprofit organization that seeks to combat teen pregnancy and sexually transmitted diseases through education. Fact sheets answer teens' questions on hepatitis B and sexual health.

**The Medical Institute for Sexual Health.** "Hepatitis C." www.medinstitute.org/public/105.cfm. Fact sheet answers teens' questions on hepatitis C and sexual health.

**The Hepatitis C Trust.** "Jazzy de Lisser-HerHepatitis C Treatment Video." www.hepctrust.org.uk/treatment/videos.

# Index

# Picture Credits

Cover Photo: 4designersart/ Shutterstock.com

Adam Gault / Photo Researchers, Inc., 81

AJPhoto / Photo Researchers, Inc., 54

© Andrew Cowie / Alamy, 40

AP Photo/Paul Sakuma, 73

AP Photo/Victoria Will, 78

© Bill Bachmann / Alamy, 75

BSIP / Photo Researchers, Inc., 33

© Chad Ehlers / Alamy, 38

© David Lee / Alamy, 69

Ed Clark/Time Life Pictures/ Getty Images, 48

Garo / Phanie / Photo Researchers, Inc., 63

Garry Watson / Photo Researchers, Inc., 25

Gary Retherford / Photo Researchers, Inc., 61

© Golden Pixels LLC/Alamy, 20

Hank Morgan / Photo Researchers, Inc., 90

Henny Allis / Photo Researchers, Inc., 84

Ian Hooton / Photo Researchers, Inc., 50

Jim Dowdalls / Photo Researchers, Inc., 97

Jim Varney / Photo Researchers, Inc., 66

© Keith Morris / Alamy, 36

Keystone/Hulton Archive/ Getty Images, 32

Mark Thomas / Photo Researchers, Inc., 42

Monica Schroeder / Science Source / Photo Researchers, Inc., 93

Olivier Voisin / Photo Researchers, Inc., 59

Phanie / Photo Researchers, Inc., 88

Philippe Garo / Photo Researchers, Inc., 56

Primal Pictures / Photo Researchers, Inc., 23

Publiphoto / Photo Researchers, Inc., 29

Rajau / Phanie / Photo Researchers, Inc., 70

© Richard Levine / Alamy, 9

© Tony Cordoza / Alamy, 44

© Walter McBride/Corbis, 11

Will & Deni McIntyre / Photo Researchers, Inc., 27

# About the Author

Melissa Abramovitz has been writing books, magazine articles, poems, and short stories for children, teenagers, and adults for twenty-five years. Many of her works are on medical and health topics.

She grew up in San Diego, California, and developed an interest in medical topics as a teenager. At one time she thought she wanted to become a doctor, but she earned a degree in psychology from the University of California, San Diego in 1976 and went on to become a writer.